maTch

maTch

A Systematic, Sane Process
for Hiring the
Right Person Every Time

DAN ERLING

WILEY

John Wiley & Sons, Inc.

Published by John Wiley & Sons, Inc., Hoboken, New Jersey.
Published simultaneously in Canada.

For general information on our other products and services or for technical support, please contact our Customer Care Department within the United States at (800) 762-2974, outside the United States at (317) 572-3993 or fax (317) 572-4002.

Wiley also publishes its books in a variety of electronic formats. Some content that appears in print may not be available in electronic books. For more information about Wiley products, visit our web site at www.wiley.com.

Library of Congress Cataloging-in-Publication Data:

ISBN 978-0-470-87898-9 (cloth)

ISBN 978-0-470-93970-3 (ebk)

ISBN 978-0-470-93971-0 (ebk)

ISBN 978-1-118-01461-5 (ebk)

Printed in the United States of America

10 9 8 7 6 5 4 3 2 1

To my dad and business partner Bert Erling,
who taught me how to make lemonade.

CONTENTS

PREFACE THE AWAKENING   ix

ACKNOWLEDGMENTS   xv

Introduction   1

MATCH   The Foundation   7

Chapter 1   Assume the Proper Mind-Set   9

Chapter 2   Begin with the Mission   17

Chapter 3   Assemble the Hiring Team   26

Chapter 4   Clarify the Corporate Culture   32

MATCH   The Process   39

Phase I—Preparing the Recruiting Plan

Chapter 5   Create the Organizational Chart: Step 1   41

Chapter 6   Compile a Job Overview: Step 2   47

Chapter 7   Create the Competency Profile: Step 3   55

Chapter 8   Structure the Recruiting Plan: Step 4   77

MATCH   The Process   89

Phase II—Implementing the Recruiting Plan

Chapter 9   Conduct the Phone Screen: Step 5   91

Chapter 10   Conduct the Face-to-Face Interview: Step 6   102

Chapter 11   Check References: Step 7   119

Chapter 12   Perform Background Checks: Step 8   128

MATCH   The Process   131

Phase III—Executing the Hire

Chapter 13   Make the Decision: Step 9   133

Chapter 14   Extend the Offer: Step 10   137

Chapter 15   Receive Acceptance: Step 11   142

Chapter 16   Perform Onboarding: Step 12   146

MATCH   The Process   153

Phase IV—Following Up

Chapter 17   Retain the Employee: Step 13   155

Chapter 18   Test the Return on Investment: Step 14   162

Chapter 19   Make the Process Stick: Step 15   169

Chapter 20   Foster a Culture of Effective Hiring: Step 16   177

CONCLUSION   183

APPENDIX I   A Word about Contractors   189

APPENDIX II   Sample Documents for Hiring a Controller   193

APPENDIX III   The Cost of a Mishire: The Story of the Bad Controller   201

APPENDIX IV   Onboarding Checklist   207

ABOUT THE AUTHOR   213

INDEX   217

PREFACE

The Awakening

A $150 million public company had just moved from the West Coast to Atlanta. Like many technology companies in 2001, their business situation had changed dramatically. In the heyday of the dot-com explosion, their stock traded at $125 per-share; now it was trading at $0.12. At least they weren't out of business. In fact, a nifty piece of technology gave them great hope.

Those who saw the potential in this company included the new chief financial officer (CFO)—a brilliant professional with lots of energy, street smarts, and an uncanny knack for helping those around him reach beyond their capabilities. In addition to being technically adept in all aspects of finance, the CFO had an uncommon combination of humor and humility, which helped him gain the trust and respect of his team. The chief executive officer (CEO) took notice, giving the CFO the responsibility of, first, keeping the financial ship from sinking, and second, getting the ship repaired and back on course.

The difficulties of the post-9/11 economy and the dot-com bust were further exacerbated by the move from the West Coast to Atlanta. Bad timing, indeed. A few key employees had relocated with the company, but the majority were new. Old and new alike were quickly becoming demoralized. An organization that was already spiraling downward was further damaged by a rushed and erratic hiring process.

The new CFO had a monumental task ahead of him as he took the reins. Last year, his company was the darling of the investment world; now, it was on the verge of dying completely. The staff he inherited had been hastily cobbled together rather than carefully selected. The accounting department was missing quarterly deadlines, and the Atlanta business newspaper was spreading bad PR across the city. Word on the street was negative—top talent had no interest in joining a company in such disarray.

Fast forward to the present: this company is a darling of the investment world, with analysts bragging about the rebound of a resilient company. The corporate culture is one of accomplishment and success, and the accounting department hasn't missed a deadline since the new CFO took the stage. The company recently went through a successful merger, purchasing a competitor to augment their service line.

What happened to transport this company from dog to darling? The answer is simple—the CFO put the right people into the right jobs. How he did it was astoundingly complicated and difficult to execute.

Serving as an executive recruiter, I had the honor of serving this great business leader as he hired his team. In terms of my career, the timing could not have been better. I was experienced enough to provide value through my recruiting energies, but this also marked my first experience in exclusively helping to create an entire department. The metamorphosis under this exceptional leader was awe inspiring.

To say I was extremely proud to be part of this hiring initiative would be an understatement, which is why I was even prouder to receive the following letter from that CFO (which I include here in its entirety):

As Chief Financial Officer, I was given six months to correct a financial organization that was a perceived weakness with the Company by all who were familiar with the Company. As such, I assessed the situation and noted several weaknesses in the staffing and the structure. I then decided to call Dan Erling to discuss my challenges and findings.

Dan came over to my Company and he listened and he observed. He understood my challenges. So I decided to hire him as a Recruiter—bringing me accounting and finance professionals. Most recruiters would have left my office and sent me some résumés. But not Dan Erling and his team at Accountants One. They went much further to ensure my success.

They got to know me. They talked to people I had worked with previously. They learned my strengths as well as my weaknesses. They did all of this so that they could find the best people—people to make me successful.

Over the next three weeks the Accountants One team only sent me a small number of résumés. I was confused, as most recruiters would always send me roughly twenty résumés per position with the hope that two or three could be interviewed. I asked why Accountants One was not following that traditional process. They told me that they only send me people who will help me succeed.

I interviewed the candidates they sent. Sure enough, they were correct. I received candidates who wanted to work for someone like me, in the industry I am in, and who needed my type of leadership for their own success. We were quickly able to hire and fill our positions.

Since that time, my organization has evolved into one of the most efficient and reliable organizations in the Company. In fact, we have done so well that we have been given the IT and the purchasing groups to manage as well. During all of this time, Dan Erling contacted my new employees and me. He checks in. He wants to make sure that everything is going as planned. He is always ready to help on any issues, and he does not do this for another fee. He only does this so his customers are satisfied.

I have never experienced such caring service from any recruiting agency during my twenty-two year career! The Accountants One recruiters significantly enhance anyone's organization because of their skill set and, most importantly, because of their caring approach.

I would never dare make the claim that our recruiting process or my work was responsible for this company's turnaround. It is clear that the success was the direct result of a great leader believing in me and allowing me to play an important role in the development of his team. However, this experience changed my life. I began to constantly think about ways to increase value through hiring strategies.

If executive recruiting had been my job, it was now my career. If it had ever been a means to an end, it was now my passion. After receiving that letter from the CFO I was hooked on the concept of maximizing the impact of people upon an organization. This was the start of my awakening, and the beginning of the process that is carefully laid out in this book.

Creating a Process

I have always been interested in data analysis. While studying math in college, my favorite courses dealt with using numbers for trending and predicting. As I grew as an executive recruiter, I began to wonder if I could apply some of these analytical concepts to the arena of hiring.

So, I began collecting data—what worked, what didn't work. The 40-year-old recruiting and staffing firm where I work acted as the perfect laboratory, allowing me to access and analyze literally thousands of hires. Over the years, I observed and documented best practices—constantly driven to create a system that would guarantee a successful hire and bring more value to my clients.

During the developmental stages I gravitated toward clients that were equally fanatical about hiring success. I began sharing results with them, and many of them applied the techniques that I was collecting. This allowed me even more points of data to observe.

There were times when I got frustrated with clients that didn't want to hear about best practices. As a person who grew up believing that "the customer is always right," I have worked for clients that demanded a less-than-optimal hiring process. But more often than not, I have had the pleasure of helping organizations improve their hiring systems and make great hires.

By establishing these best practices into our recruiting firms, our results have been phenomenal. I have been tracking the success rate at Accountants One and the Waters Organization since 2003. In 2009, our success rate was 93 percent on the direct hire (permanent) side. In 2007 and 2008, our success rate was 98 percent. I am extremely proud of these results in an industry where 60 percent is considered acceptable.

Our contract (temp) team also reaps the benefits of a systematic hiring process. In 2008 and 2009, our success rate was 88 percent, while in 2007 we were at 91 percent. Please remember that it is not unusual for our contract team to get a call at 8:30 AM for a person to report to a client at 10 AM. With that demand for speed, I am sure you will agree that this success rate is nothing short of outstanding.

Please note that I am not attempting to "sell" recruiting services; rather, my point is to share with you the objective difference in applying a process. After all, if we can achieve these stellar results at a recruiting and staffing firm, imagine the impact that this process can have on your company.

Objectivity matters a great deal to me. My intent throughout the MATCH process is to provide you not with my opinion, but rather with a documented system that has been proven over and over again in the hiring marketplace. I hope this objectivity comes through in this book.

This collection of best practices may have been inspired by the earlier letter from the CFO, but those words were just the catalyst.

So many others have been helpful in sharing their best practices. For all this help I am very thankful.

I am sure that through the publication of this book I will continue to learn from those who are dedicated to the art of hiring great people. To this point I have created a blog at www.danerling .com/blog. I welcome you to visit this site and share your thoughts with others who are passionate about hiring the right people.

ACKNOWLEDGMENTS

I would like to thank the following people for their help with this book:

Dylan Williams, for his efforts to make me a better writer by instilling in me the notion that good writing requires re-writing (and then re-writing again). I appreciate your friendship and belief in me. If I have any talent with the written word, you are to thank. You are a great friend.

My exceptional team at Accountants One and The Waters Organization, for your undying support on the path we chose and stuck to during extraordinarily difficult times. I couldn't ask for a better group of people. Thanks for going the extra mile in all you do.

Randi Bates, my remarkable marketing manager, who keeps me on task no matter how chaotic our worlds become.

The folks at John Wiley & Sons, Inc., for their patience and guidance.

My business mentors—especially Dave Buckel—who has consistently and selflessly gone out of his way to help me grow.

All the clients and candidates that I have served and will continue to serve as an executive recruiter. Thanks for putting up with my endless questions, my drive for perfection, and my occasionally unconventional approach.

Steve Meadows, who suggested the title for the book.

Pete Ori, who taught me the utility and beauty of mathematics.

Jeff Morrow, who read an early version of this book and gave me great, constructive feedback.

My dad and business partner, Bert Erling, whom we lost in May of 2010. I'm sorry that you are not around to share in the excitement of this first book. There is some comfort in knowing that so much of your philosophy and approach live on in these pages.

My mom, Carolyn Erling, who, among so many other things, taught me that when it rains at the amusement park, you can still have a great time.

My extended family, who occupy a deep and significant space in my heart, especially Carolyn Hall, who disproves every mother-in-law joke ever told.

And finally, my wonderful wife Michelle and my kids Nelson and Wren. Thanks for putting up with all the extra work that went into this endeavor. But even more importantly, thank you for being the center of my life.

MATCH

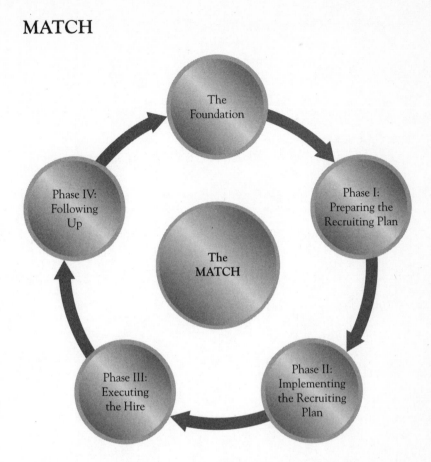

As you can see in this diagram, the MATCH process encompasses the full life cycle of hiring, from setting up a solid foundation through the hiring process itself, proceeding to a follow-up process that ensures your return on investment, and culminating in a best practices feedback loop. The MATCH sits in the center of this step-by-step logically driven process. As we progress through each section, you'll see that each circle enlarges to reveal steps towards hiring the right person for your organization.

INTRODUCTION

As president of a recruiting firm, I've been intimately involved in literally thousands of hiring decisions. I've worked with hundreds of department managers, HR professionals, and everyone whose title begins with "Chief." When I talk to them about their hiring success rate, I'm surprised at how many times I hear the same things:

> You can't find good help. . . . People are unpredictable—hiring is a crapshoot. . . . People just want a paycheck—they don't care about my company. . . . Some folks are really good at interviewing, but when you hire them, they can't do the job. . . . I found a guy with the right skills, but no one in the department likes him. . . . Young people just don't have the work ethic . . . and on and on.

What surprises me even more is how many companies accept mediocre hiring results as the norm. It doesn't occur to them that, in fact, there is a process that virtually guarantees hiring the right person every time.

Let me repeat that: *there is a process that virtually guarantees hiring the right person every time.*

That's what this book is about.

Most companies are terrible (or at least inconsistent) at hiring. This is not a good thing at all, since talent matters perhaps

1

most of all. One of my heroes, Peter Drucker, said it best when he wrote:

> The ability to make good decisions regarding people represents one of the last reliable sources of competitive advantage, since very few organizations are very good at it.

Study after study tells us that the most successful companies are those run by leaders who understand that *people* are the most important part of the business equation. In business surveys, CEOs rank having the right person in the right job as their highest concern. And business experts consistently agree that getting the right people "on the bus" is the key to an organization's success.

Despite these numerous reminders, many companies don't prioritize the hire. We just don't have time to install and work a systematic process for hiring. Business poll after business poll tells us that one third of people are miserable in their jobs, one third of people would leave their job given another opportunity, and one third of people like their jobs. How can we, as hiring managers, align people to our companies with greater expertise?

Since 1998 I have been actively involved in the world of recruiting. I am the president of Accountants One, a forty-year-old recruiting firm focusing on recruiting accounting and financial professionals. I started my career placing temporary accountants, and moved up to doing retained exclusive searches for controllers, vice presidents, and CFOs. I am also a minority partner in the Waters Organization, which is a woman-owned firm specializing in administrative placement. During my tenure in recruiting and staffing, I've carefully tracked successes and failures, compiling a structured hiring process comprised of the most effective proven hiring techniques. The MATCH process is the culmination of these best practices.

MATCH

MATCH offers a systematic and sane approach to hiring. The process works equally well for a small company hiring a controller to a large public company hiring a CFO. The MATCH process works with companies that need to add one permanent hire or an HR department charged with hiring 100 project-based contractors. At first glance, the process may look overly time consuming. In practice, however, this approach will save you a *lot* of time (and money) by dramatically increasing the efficiency of your hiring efforts. By implementing the MATCH process you will undoubtedly spend more time on the front end of the search, but you will avoid the countless wasted hours that come with hiring the wrong person.

Systematic/Sane?

I have touted the MATCH hiring process as being a "systematic/ sane approach to hiring the right person every time." Just leafing through the pages of the book, noting the step-by-step directions and carefully documented diagrams, should clarify the "systematic" nature of this approach. But why "sane"?

The answer is that with so many things on our plates, I wanted to create a hiring system that was effective but also implementable by the busiest business leader.

I have seen many business processes that require consultants to implement. This is not the case with the MATCH hiring process. Certainly, this system will take discipline to execute, but it has been designed to be "sane" in the implementation process. I'd like to think that anyone who picks up this book—no matter how busy they are—will find a system that they can implement immediately to achieve the hiring results they desire.

How to Use This Book

MATCH has two major sections—the foundation and the process. The foundation activities focus on you, your company, and your hiring team. These activities are important because they anchor the steps of the process in solid principles. They also give you and the team that initial kick of energy to get momentum moving in your favor. The foundation activities require a bit of reflection and buy-in from others, but once you have it, you're on firm footing.

The process section details the nitty-gritty of the hire—from developing and implementing a recruiting plan through executing on the hire and fostering a culture of effective hiring. Each step builds on the previous one to keep everyone involved working efficiently and consistently toward finding the right candidate. I challenge you to complete all the steps. Even if you are tempted or pressed by time to cut corners—don't. Once you've been through the full process once or twice, the time savings and quality improvement will be blindingly obvious. The first time through, however, some activities may appear less important than others.

Frequently Asked Questions

The following are some questions you might be asking yourself.

What kind of success can I expect from using the MATCH Process?

At my recruiting firm, we define *success* for a permanent employee as a person who is still with a company after one year. The business hiring average is around 50 percent. The professional recruiters' average is not much better—around 60 percent. However, businesses and recruiting firms using the MATCH process boast success rates above 95 percent. The process works.

Is MATCH right for my organization?

Following is a quick assessment to help you gauge the health of your hiring processes. You can be as detailed as you'd like, but if nothing else, this exercise should give you a sense of your as-is state:

Assessment

1. What has been your company's hiring success rate over the past year?
2. What has been your company's retention rate over the past three years?
3. What is your current payroll to human capital return on investment (ROI) ratio?
4. What percentage of your employees are able to state the mission of your company?
5. What percentage of your employees have a working job description?
6. What percentage of your employees are in the correct role in terms of being challenged and fairly compensated?
7. What percentage of your staff match the corporate culture of your organization?
8. What percentage of your staff has a competency profile that augments the corporate dynamic?
9. How much do your current employees augment your organizational mission?
10. What is your hiring plan?
11. Who manages your hiring plan?
12. What personality attributes bring the greatest value to your organization?

Do I have to implement all the steps of MATCH?

Yes, wherever possible. Make no mistake—I'm diametrically opposed to process for the sake of process. Great companies focus on results, not systems. However, companies that attract, hire, and retain the best people implement *all* the steps of the MATCH process in some form or fashion.

Each step of the MATCH process is intended to build on the previous. By systematically moving through each step, the process is designed to increase the odds of hiring the right person. By the end of the process, you are as close to 100 percent hiring certainty as you can possibly be.

Does MATCH work across all industries?

Definitely. MATCH was cultivated in a recruiting firm—Accountants One—that has specialized in temporary and permanent placements for accounting and financial professionals since 1973. While my examples are admittedly strongly rooted in the world of accounting and finance, MATCH has proven to be effective across many disciplines, including administrative, sales, and human resources.

Why should I bother with MATCH?

The purpose of this book is to help you achieve a competitive advantage. You'll be introduced to a process with an extraordinary track record that, if followed, will ensure that you hire the best person available for your open positions. It may be tough to muster up the discipline to implement this process, but the results will be dramatic.

MATCH

The Foundation

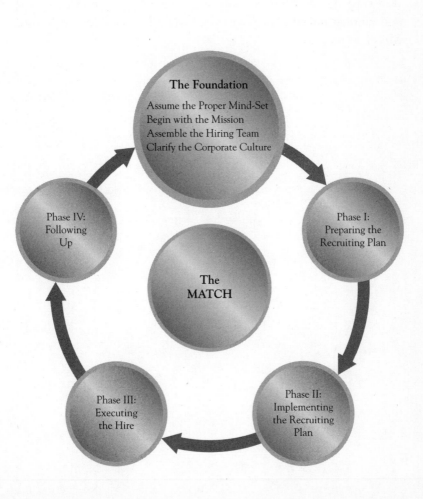

The Foundation
Assume the Proper Mind-Set
Begin with the Mission
Assemble the Hiring Team
Clarify the Corporate Culture

Phase IV:
Following
Up

Phase I:
Preparing the
Recruiting Plan

The
MATCH

Phase III:
Executing
the Hire

Phase II:
Implementing
the Recruiting
Plan

Chances are that you have more than enough to do in your "regular" job—and now you have to find time to hire someone? In addition to the daily storm of deadlines and meetings, going through the hiring process requires you to focus and amp up your energies. The Foundation steps outlined in the diagram on the previous page prepare you for this effort by first reinforcing the significance and consequence of what you're about to do. Once you have the proper mind-set, you embark on the hiring journey by beginning with the mission. You'll then assemble the hiring team using the mission as your foundation. Next, you will clarify the corporate culture, exploring how to most effectively express the mission of the organization through that culture. With your Foundation solidly in place and momentum in your favor, you'll then be ready to execute the MATCH process.

1

Assume the Proper Mind-Set

Greatness is not a function of circumstance. Greatness, it turns out, is largely a matter of conscious choice, and discipline.

—Jim Collins

Get ready—because whether this is your first hire or your 150th, whether you're hiring a chief financial officer (CFO) or an accounts payable clerk, a salesperson or an information technology (IT) manager, a mail clerk or a chief information officer (CIO)—*all hires count*. A great hire will keep your organization profitable, growing and happy, whereas a poor hire will drain your company of morale, time, and profits. Hiring directly and indirectly affects your bottom line. You need to keep that top of mind as we explore the five components of the proper mind-set.

Sticky Notes:

• Nothing is more important than hiring the right people.

• Guard against believing you're a great judge of people.

• Hiring great people requires discipline.

• Implementing the MATCH process will dramatically impact your bottom line.

1. **Make hiring your main concern.**

Prioritize hiring—consider it as your most critical activity until it's complete. You generally do well at those things you prioritize, so do the same for this activity.

Need a little boost of inspiration before we get into all the details of the MATCH process? Let's look at a couple of quotes. I consider these thoughts to constitute the basis of the proper mind-set you'll to need to hire at the 95+ percent success rate:

From Jack Welch:

> Hiring good people is hard. Hiring great people is brutally hard. And yet nothing matters more in winning than getting the right people on the field.

From Peter Drucker:

> People decisions are the ultimate—perhaps the only—control of an organization. People determine the performance capacity of an organization. No organization can do better than the people it has. The yield from the human resource really determines the organization's performance. And that's decided by the basic people decisions: whom we hire and whom we fire, where we place people, and whom we promote. The quality of these human decisions largely determines whether the organization is being run seriously, whether its mission, its values, and its objectives are real and meaningful to people, rather than just public relations and rhetoric.

In a practical sense, preparing to make a hire—*especially* if hiring is not your main responsibility—means that you must treat the process as a critical-path project. Plan hiring activities as if they were meetings on your calendar, and stick to your commitments. To the degree possible, gear down on other projects until you're through with hiring. If nothing else, prioritize this hire on the same level as your most pressing project. Get serious about it—your company's well-being is riding on it!

2. **Stop believing you're a "great judge of people."**

Ouch. I know; this one can hurt. I mean, who doesn't think they're at least a *decent* judge of people? I myself have participated in literally thousands of hiring decisions. I'm usually able to spot talent and nuances and potential issues that never even occur to the average executive involved in hiring. However, whenever I begin to get full of myself for being so "people savvy," I'm reminded of another Peter Drucker quote:

"Any executive who starts out believing that he or she is a good judge of people is going to end up making the worst decisions. To be a judge of people is not a power given to mere mortals. Those who have a batting average of almost a thousand in such decisions start out with a very simple premise: that they are not judges of people. . . . An executive, too, has to learn not to depend on insight and knowledge of people but on a mundane, boring, and conscientious step-by-step process."

So, take it from Mr. Drucker and do your best to suspend personal judgment. Though it may sound harsh, what you consider "being a good judge of people" is often just a case of mild narcissism. We humans tend to connect with people similar to us. That's natural, and it even has a place in the hiring process. However, you must be very careful not to subconsciously cut a favored candidate a break when deciding if they fit the position's requirements. Stick to the parameters you've set for the role instead of re-creating the position to fit their strengths.

When you're given an employee to manage, you must play to their strengths; when you hire a person, stick to your requirements as closely as possible. If a person doesn't exactly fit the bill, but you believe that he or she would make a valuable hire, step away and reevaluate the hire. Will you be sacrificing payroll dollars and achieving only half your objective, or will this person bring value in other areas? What I am advocating is that you go into the hire with your eyes wide open—not swayed by personality dynamics.

A CEO and friend of mine hired a public relations (PR) manager a few years ago. This CEO really "liked" this new employee; they'd definitely clicked during the interview. There was just one hiccup: the PR manager hated talking to the press. She had gotten burned with bad exposure a few times in a previous job, and as a result, she focused almost exclusively on writing, a medium with which she felt very comfortable. In terms of meeting business objectives for the company—in this case, increasing brand awareness—she was only doing half of the job.

If my CEO friend had been looking for a PR manager that specialized exclusively in writing, he would have hired the right person. Unfortunately, his organization needed expertise in both writing and talking to the press. Even with coaching, the hire wound up being a disaster. My friend was unhappy, and the PR manager wound up resigning.

Deciding if a person can actually *do* the job requires detaching yourself in an almost scientific, objective manner and working through a defined process. Had the CEO followed this process, he would have discovered this shortcoming in the PR manager. At that point he could have either rewritten the job description or made the decision to continue the search for a PR manager with strengths in both writing *and* communicating to the press.

When most people hear the phrase "hiring the wrong person," they think of the oddball who doesn't fit in with the office culture, or complains all the time, or is chronically late. Yes, clearly, those are signs of a bad hire and poor judgment by the hiring team. However, what many people do not consider is that a poor hire can also be the person who *does* fit in with the team, is optimistic and on time, but who doesn't help fulfill business objectives. They do work that "fits their personality" rather than the work that *needs* to be done to keep you growing and profitable. Following a systematic process helps you avoid this uncomfortable situation.

A formal hiring process allows a company to become objective in its hiring, which is critical:

- **If *you're* the one making the decision.** Face it—we all have biases, and we all have blind spots. If you're in charge of this hiring decision, your credibility with the rest of your staff is on the line. You must have a way of removing your objectivity from the process so that you can make the best decision possible.
- **If you're one member of a team that's making the decision.** The team must work from a common perspective to make sure all the bases are covered and that each member knows his or her role. Those parts must complement each other so that when decision time comes, everyone is working from the same set of criteria.

3. **Commit to the MATCH process.**

Okay, now you have an inkling of what you're in for. I'm going to lay out the hiring process for you, task by task. If followed properly, this process will get you as close to a 100 percent success rate as possible. And yes, it *is* mundane. It takes discipline, and it takes time that you don't think you have. And if you shortcut the process—if you cherry-pick certain tasks and ignore others—you *will* get burned.

If one of the new recruiters in my firm gets in a slump, we review their compliance with this process in detail. I invariably find that they're shortcutting some task because they think it's (pick one) *tough to do/time consuming/boring/unnecessary*. Once corrected, however, they perform better, and they become more committed to the entire process.

While the process is demanding, it doesn't require superhuman talent to carry out. What it requires more than anything is for you to make hiring the best people your priority. The process also requires a little bit of faith—at least the first time through—to see how the whole thing comes together and how the latter steps are affected by the earlier steps. And remember, I'll help you through it. I've been through this process thousands of times, and have seen great things happen as a result.

4. **Suspend your gut instincts.**

The biggest blind spot hiring managers have in our recruiting experience is that they believe that their "intuition" will guide them to the correct hire. They look at a strict process as being "cold," time consuming, or just not worth the effort. They'll often cherry-pick parts of the process—the ones that make sense and/or are easy for them—and avoid the more uncomfortable or difficult steps.

Entrepreneurs are especially susceptible to making bad hiring decisions. For one thing, they're insanely busy. For another, their "gut" has gotten them where they are today. Many times their success has been due in part to their ability to make a leap (or several leaps) of faith.

Why doesn't that leap of faith work in the hiring process? Well, the words *leap* and *faith* might be a clue! But all kidding aside—the reason you must follow a strict process is that it's the best way to keep you aligned with your business mission, and aligning with your business mission keeps you profitable. At the end of the day—even if you're *completely* comfortable with the person you hired—you're in trouble if they cannot fulfill your business objectives within the framework of your mission.

By the way, note that I am advocating that you *suspend* your gut instincts, not *ignore*. Over years of observation I have noted that your intuition will actually play a role in the final decision. By sticking to the process as objectively as you can, you will be feeding your instincts consistent and clear information, which will lessen your inner conflicts and make your decision that much easier.

5. **Ponder the bigger picture.**

If you've taken the time to read thus far about putting yourself in the proper mind-set, I should probably get right to the point: the hiring process, when done correctly, hurts. It *should* hurt, and it should be sort of boring. I say that, and I'm an executive recruiter! That's all right, though, because I know two essential things about hiring:

- When it's done right and you find the right person—a person who matches the skills needed and the culture of your company—that is a *beautiful* thing; and I don't use the word *beautiful* lightly. I have seen individuals, departments, and whole companies transformed as a result of placing the right people in the right roles. Now let's go a little bigger in scope—consider the effect of a productive, satisfied person on his or her family, community, and even the economy. The ripple effect can be enormous. Yes, a beautiful thing indeed.

- On the other hand, the cost of a mishire can be staggering—up to 13 times that person's salary. Oh, we all have a story, don't we? If you want to read mine, see Appendix III for the story of the Bad Controller. The *literal* costs to the company of a controller hired for two years, who turned out to be a mishire, were easily over $1.5 million. And that figure was just for *that one person*. What if they had hired others just like them? What about the good people who quit because they couldn't stand the guy? Yes, there's a ripple effect here, too. What about loss of department morale? Bad press? Angry customers? Getting the new person up to speed? You get the picture.

If you find the MATCH process tedious, focus on results—they will be far from boring. Done correctly, this hiring structure will impact your company in a positive way—from a multimillion-dollar impact on your bottom line to a happier, more productive team.

So, with hopes that I have caught your attention—onward we go.

Begin with the Mission

We wanted Nike to be the world's best sports and fitness company. Once you say that, you have a focus. You don't end up making wing tips or sponsoring the next Rolling Stones world tour.

—Philip Knight

The Purpose of the Mission Statement from a Hiring Perspective

I still remember the moment when the impact of the mission statement hit home. I was sitting in the audience at a business seminar. The speaker asked us to shut our eyes and point in the direction that we thought was true north. After a few moments, he asked us to open our eyes.

Fingers were pointing in every conceivable direction! Some of the participants were pointing to the front of the room, others to the back, and there were even a few who were pointing to the ceiling. There was no consistency whatsoever across the group.

This simple exercise showed me that when a group of people lack clarity, its members can interpret reality in many different ways. Of course, if the speaker had indicated true north before we closed our eyes, then our fingers would have all been aligned.

In the same way, a mission statement provides your organization with its true north. It aligns your people in the same direction and reminds them, in the simplest terms, of what you're trying to do and where you're trying to go.

Knowing—and making others aware of—your company's true north is particularly critical in this age of the information avalanche. The ceaseless barrage of noise on almost every conceivable topic can paralyze people's productivity on a daily basis. How many hours are lost clicking around web sites and/or responding to inconsequential emails? A solid strong mission allows you to quickly judge if your actions are aligned with your company's direction, neutral to it, or working against it. The mission prompts us to be *effective* rather than just *busy*.

Simply stated, you cannot build a *great* company without a mission. Great companies have a purpose that puts their people's

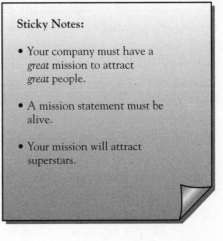

Sticky Notes:

• Your company must have a *great* mission to attract *great* people.

• A mission statement must be alive.

• Your mission will attract superstars.

energy into focus and allows them to accomplish something bigger and more substantial than just getting a paycheck.

This sense of a mission is critical to your two main categories of employees:

- **Your superstars (10 percent).** Superstars know they're valuable. They can apply their skills at your company or at your competitor's. A meaningful mission allows these "top ten percenters" to gain perspective and bragging rights around their career. They are able to see their role in a larger sense—something that lets them derive greater meaning from their performance and also acts as a retention tool.
- **Your "B" performers (70 percent).** This group really *needs* that mission clarity to keep them focused. A mission statement makes the average employee just a little bit better. Knowing true north helps them synergize their actions. For example, consider an organization with a service-oriented mission and a ringing front desk phone. An employee who is aware of that mission will be more likely to pick up the phone. By contrast, if an organization has a mission statement focused on ingenuity, that same employee may let the same call roll to voice mail, and know that they are correct in doing so. The mission helps people to understand what is most important, and therefore allows average performers to align their behaviors with the organization's overarching intent.

You may have noticed that these two bullet points cover only 80 percent of your employees. Nothing—not even a mission statement—helps the bottom 20 percent. However, utilizing your mission statement lets you quickly identify those employees not in line with the mission of the organization. The good leader will utilize the mission statement to quickly remove those who are misaligned with the company's focus.

Today's market demands creativity. When our country's economy revolved around manufacturing, all a company needed was a healthy body that could perform repetitive tasks for 30 plus years. It was quite obvious whether the person was doing his or her job—they reached quota, or did not.

But modern organizations need people to think, to innovate, and to create. It's what makes the difference, but it's very difficult to strategically manage. You can't measure how much a person is actively engaged with your company, its products, and its services. A paycheck gets you a body and certain number of agreed-upon tasks; that's it. The stuff that gives an organization a competitive advantage—the creative thoughts—are volunteered. And unless you have a mission that will capture an employee's heart, you will not have access to the full wealth of treasures that someone can bring to your company. The mission statement should capture that person's heart, mind, imagination, and energies.

From a talent acquisition perspective, working from a mission transforms the hiring process from a series of steps to an expression of the mission. It's this expression that gives the MATCH process its energy, focus, and initial push of momentum.

Thoughts on the Mission Statement Itself

As an executive recruiter, I have helped a number of companies make great hires without ever mentioning a mission. Clearly, there are very good companies that function without a clearly defined mission. But my point is that in terms of making effective hires, your odds of attracting, hiring, and retaining a great employee are enhanced if your company has taken the time to think out a meaningful and purposeful statement. Remember, the MATCH process is designed to increase your odds of hiring the right person every time, and having a clearly defined mission is a critical step in this process.

Great mission statements come in many forms. I have seen some comprised of 10 words, and others that span several pages. Some effective companies abandon the idea of the mission, and create a *mantra*—something shorter and more easily memorized. Other companies specify their core values within their mission by adding sections on values and ethics. There is no right or wrong way to construct a mission statement; all that matters is that the organization finds meaning and synergy around a single direction, just as with the exercise of pointing north as I mentioned at the beginning of this chapter.

A great mission statement should express an organization's central ideology in three core areas:

1. **Values.** These are the core values that are part of your central ideology and that remain constant. In other words, these values would be the same even if you moved into another industry. Examples of core values include concepts such as: innovation, superior customer service, integrity, and environmental responsibility.
2. **Purpose.** This is the reason your company exists, but expressed in a somewhat more idealistic way. To find your core purpose, ask yourself how you earn a profit. Then ask yourself why, and work to get at the main benefit you provide. Example: "We sell toys." Why? "To make kids happy." What makes kids happy about playing with your toys? "We engage children's imagination." Engage? "We engage and develop children's imagination." Okay . . . now you're on the path to finding your core purpose.
3. **Goals.** Jim Collins calls these the "BHAGS—big, hairy, audacious goals." You may only have a 50 percent chance of achieving these—but by golly, you're on your way! These are goals like "become number 1 in our market," or "provide a PC for every child" or "be bigger than Microsoft."

These three categories provide the foundation you need for a solid mission.

Ownership of Mission

Mission statements should be the concern—and work—of every one of your company's employees. That's the only way to guarantee buy-in and make it a "living" statement. Nothing disenfranchises employees quite like knowing that while only one or two people developed the mission, everyone is supposed to follow it.

If you don't have a mission statement, a good way to create one is to survey your personnel on the three categories previously mentioned. Hold focus groups to brainstorm and gain buy-in. Even better—get your customers involved. Their perspective, especially in the area of visionary goals, can be quite eye-opening.

Remember to maintain a sense of pride as you complete this task; after all, your mission statement should make you and your people proud of what they do and proud of the values they promote. But be careful that it's not *so* highfalutin that your people feel disconnected from it. The mission statement should not drain your people, nor should it be flat: it should energize!

In my opinion the *best* mission statement created by *any* organization is that of the renowned luxury hotel chain the Ritz-Carlton. To see the impact of their mission just visit any of their hotels. The mystique perforates the walls in ways that cannot be bought—all fostered by stories like the one a friend likes to tell.

This friend was staying in a Ritz hotel over several days, during which time he was doing a great deal of writing. The desk-chair in his room was a nonadjustable/one-size-fits-all model—comfortable, but not designed for marathon writing sessions. He buzzed down to the front desk and asked for a more ergonomic chair. The friendly staff quickly showed up with an adjustable chair, and soon he was writing in a much more comfortable manner.

He chalked up this experience to the Ritz-Carlton standard and soon forgot about it until a month later when he checked into a Ritz in a different part of the country. You can imagine how blown away he was when he walked into his room to find an adjustable chair at his desk. The staff had noted his preference and proactively accommodated his need for another writing session. Now *that* is service.

SAMPLE MISSION STATEMENTS

Below are a few examples of mission statements from some well-known, profitable organizations:

"To organize the world's information and make it universally accessible and useful."

—Google

"Dedication to the highest quality of Customer Service delivered with a sense of warmth, friendliness, individual pride, and Company Spirit."

—Southwest Airlines

"To unleash the potential and power of people and organizations for the common good."

—Ken Blanchard Companies

"The mission of the Walt Disney Company is to be one of the world's leading producers and providers of entertainment and information. Using our portfolio of brands to differentiate our content, services and consumer products, we seek to develop the most creative, innovative and profitable entertainment experiences and related products in the world."

—The Walt Disney Company

"We fulfill dreams through the experience of motorcycling, by providing to motorcyclists and to the general public an expanding line of motorcycles and branded products and services in selected market segments."

—Harley-Davidson, Inc.

A Portion of the Ritz-Carlton Mission Statement

The Credo

The Ritz-Carlton Hotel is a place where the genuine care and comfort of our guests is our highest mission.

We pledge to provide the finest personal service and facilities for our guests who will always enjoy a warm, relaxed, yet refined ambience.

The Ritz-Carlton experience enlivens the senses, instills well-being, and fulfills even the unexpressed wishes and needs of our guests.

Motto

At The Ritz-Carlton Hotel Company, LLC, "We are ladies and gentlemen serving ladies and gentlemen." This motto exemplifies the anticipatory service provided by all staff members.

Three Steps of Service

1. A warm and sincere greeting. Use the guest name, if and when possible.
2. Anticipation and compliance with guest needs.
3. Fond farewell. Give them a warm good-bye and use their names, if and when possible.

I hope that I have made it clear that the mission statement is a powerful tool in capturing the hearts and minds of both present and future employees. Use your mission statement as an initial step in the hiring process and you will be on the way to creating a rock solid foundation. With that mission statement at the helm of your efforts, proceed to the next step in the hiring process—assembling the hiring team.

Avoid the Dilbert Web Site Mission Statement

On office refrigerators across the globe, you'll more than likely find a Dilbert cartoon. This extremely popular comic strip examines the absurd side of business. On the Dilbert web site (www.dilbert.com) there used to be a very funny mission statement generator.

After choosing a list of adverbs, verbs, adjectives, and nouns the generator gave you such great-sounding nonsense as:

- "Our goal is to completely utilize business deliverables so that we may professionally revolutionize professional intellectual capital to exceed customer expectations."
- "Our mission is to assertively create business meta-services."
- "Our challenge is to collaboratively fashion prospective products so that we may efficiently coordinate business solutions."

- "The customer can count on us to globally customize effective sources so that we may authoritatively facilitate prospective solutions to set us apart from the competition."

Despite the fact that I don't know what *any* of those statements mean, I've come across many similar-sounding ones in company brochures or neatly framed in the offices of CEOs during my travels.

Does your company have a mission statement? If so, is it "living"? That is, can your employees recite it? Does it affect your strategy and your day-to-day decisions? If not, then you may just have a collection of adverbs, verbs, adjectives, and nouns masquerading as a mission.

3

Assemble the Hiring Team

Most discussions of decision making assume that only senior executives make decisions or that only senior executives' decisions matter. This is a dangerous mistake.

—Peter Drucker

G rowth of an organization will be most impactful if employees hired to execute are banded together first and foremost through the organization's mission. In other words, employees perform most effectively if they are naturally motivated by what the company does and how they do it. Organizations that are most successful in their hiring process understand this truth.

But how does a company express its mission through a hire? A key ingredient is developing a mission-driven hiring team. This chapter will explore the development of that team.

Sticky Notes:

- A *great* hire starts at the top of an organization.

- Assign specific duties to the hiring team.

- The best hiring teams are formed around the mission statement.

Who Leads the Charge?

Great hiring starts at the top. The most successful organizations are passionate in their belief of the following: (1) hiring the right people is critical in maintaining competitive advantage, and (2) the CEO (or business leader) sets an organization's hiring tone. If the CEO is wildly passionate about hiring great people, then the organization will reflect this same ideal. If the CEO doesn't care, then neither will the organization.

The Hiring Team

When a position opens up, most companies pull together to interview, evaluate, and hire a new employee. This team is organized around the assumption that the company needs to hire someone. Most often, this team has little direction and less structure. They choose the best candidate they can, and then disband when the position is filled.

The MATCH process advocates the development of a more permanent **hiring team** responsible for upholding the company's mission above and beyond the hiring of a specific individual. This means that the hiring team acts in a broader manner by reviewing the open position in the context of the company mission, and then proceeding in a structured manner.

On the front end of the process, the hiring team explores the underlying reasons for the hire. On the back end of the process—after the candidate has been employed—the hiring team is responsible for testing the return on investment, reviewing the hiring process, and generally promoting a culture that supports the process of effective hiring. In this sense, the hiring team is responsible for much more than simply recruiting.

Hiring Team Roles

In a large company, I have seen hiring teams of more than a dozen people. I have also seen small entrepreneurial endeavors where the hiring team consisted of one person playing all the parts. Whatever the case, a successful hiring team must have coverage in each of the following categories:

Leader (e.g., CEO, president, and/or department head)— responsible for:

- Choosing the team
- Conveying importance of entire hiring process

- Speaking to department heads about freeing up team members' time, if necessary
- Leading discussions around the value of the hire, return on investment, and how to make the process stick
- Acting as decision tie-breaker
- Developing the initial job description
- Approving the recruiting plan

Administrators (admin and/or human resources [HR])—responsible for:

- Managing paperwork and administration
- Coordinating team actions:
  o Scheduling meetings
  o Compiling the skills and competency questionnaires
  o Administering the recruiting plan
  o Time keeping (while a hire should never be rushed, it's critical to stick to allocated meeting times)

Recruiters (department head and/or HR)—responsible for:

- Assessing the team's training needs
- Sourcing Talent
- Training others (or oneself) on interviewing techniques
- Assigning interviewers
- Coordinating structure of interviews—team or individual

Interviewers (department head, HR, peers, subordinates, key members of directly related departments—e.g., for a director of fixed assets, have a person from the tax department interview them)—responsible for:

- Providing input to skills and competency questionnaires
- Doing the actual interviewing:
  o High-level phone screen
  o In-depth skills interview
  o Competency interview

Review the four types of roles above and decide which person or persons should be chosen for each. And remember—no one in your company is just sitting around idly, waiting to become part of a hiring team. They're busy doing their jobs. In fact, the people in the department with the open position may be unusually busy trying to compensate for the missing resources. Getting everyone on board might require a bit of a negotiation, but being a member of the hiring team should be considered an important responsibility. Participation should be mandatory, except in clearly justifiable cases.

Assembling the Team

Once the team has been chosen, they need to meet. As tempting as it will be to launch into the action plan, spend time making sure the team has the proper mind-set. Focus the group on the importance of hiring the best people, and reinforce the need to make a quality decision based on the company's mission.

In addition, commit to the *process*. Work the process as thoroughly and objectively as possible. Guard against the notion that you're a "great judge of character." Don't go on gut instinct. Remind them that you're a team, and *everyone's* opinion counts. Everyone is expected to be engaged with the process: Be thorough. Take notes. Be humble, but assert your points. Listen. Play fair.

Always have your company's mission statement available for review. Go over it with the team. The hiring process should serve as a catalyst to reinforce and express that very mission.

Meeting Agenda

Begin your first hiring team meeting with a welcome, help put the team in the proper mind-set, and review the company mission. After the welcome, the other areas to cover on the agenda include the following:

- **Justifying the position.** Review the open position with regard to the mission, the company direction, and the department's needs. Do you need to fill the position? Do you need more than one? Should this position be filled by someone already in the department? Will that create a new opening?

- **Assigning the roles.** Review the list of roles and responsibilities. Remember, a person can be assigned multiple roles, provided they can handle the load. Make sure each person is clear on the commitment they're being asked to make.
- **Reviewing the hiring process.** Review the MATCH process graphic with the entire team to get everyone on the same page. Encourage them to get any questions out in the open.
- **Planning any training.** Plan to hold training on interviewing techniques, legal issues, the MATCH process, note-taking, and so on, for anyone new to the process.
- **Completing the company and department culture scorecard.** See the next chapter for details on this. In addition to helping the team gain more clarity about the company, completing the scorecard is a lively team-building exercise.

A warning against politics: as with any group, political agendas can creep in, especially once the real work of the hiring process begins. Be on guard against this natural tendency. The effective group leader must constantly remind the team that they are together for the organization's greater good.

I'm reminded of a case where a CEO assembled her hiring team only to find that after two weeks the group was still discussing roles—politics and pettiness had taken over. The CEO had to get involved, reassigning leadership and reclarifying goals. She spent time reminding the hiring team to become selfless in their extraordinarily important objective. After this restart, the hiring team became charged with their role—this led to a *great* hire in less than a month.

Clarify the Corporate Culture

If you build that foundation, both the moral and the ethical foundation, as well as the business foundation, and the experience foundation, then the building won't crumble.

—Henry Kravis

W hile your mission statement conveys your values, purpose, and daring goals, your company expresses that mission through its culture. In order to hire someone that augments that mission, your hiring team must clearly understand that culture.

What is your company's approach to, say, deadlines? Will people work overtime to meet a deadline, or does the deadline move to accommodate people's schedules? And how do people normally communicate—by email? Phone? Instant message? Personal one-on-one conversations? For that matter, how much do people talk about their home lives while at work? All of these answers speak to the state of your company's culture.

Sticky Notes:

- Assess your company's culture using the scorecard.

- Assess the culture of the candidate's department.

- Compare company and department cultural assessments.

Corporate culture is extraordinarily difficult to measure but imperative in making a great hire. This difficulty arises because you sit in the middle of your corporate culture every day. It's like trying to get a fish to describe the ocean—unless you have seen land to compare it to, the ocean just simply *is*.

Your Hiring Team and the Scorecard

I hope by this point you've recognized that I am a hiring pragmatist. The MATCH process is an objective collection of best practices designed to ensure a successful hire. The tools suggested for moving through any section of the MATCH process are *not* canons chiseled in granite. After a decade of observing ineffective and effective hiring practices, I have come to recognize that what matters most are the systematic steps, not the techniques and tools within those steps.

In that light, when it comes to evaluating corporate culture, I have found that it doesn't matter how you do it—just that you do it. There are many tools for evaluating the culture of an organization. I have seen some practices that require several weeks of consulting expertise. By contrast, the method I tout takes just a few minutes to implement.

Should the hiring team decide to use my suggested method, then ideally, everyone in a company should fill out the scorecard. Responses should be anonymous; however, they should be separated departmentally. By doing this you will be able to more effectively align your new hire with the cultural differences that exist from department to department.

Should it not be feasible to have the cultural scorecard completed by everyone in the company, then compromise by having it filled out only by the department with the open position. In almost every instance where I have helped a company implement this scorecard, the results have proven to be surprising to the leadership team. They expect the culture to align with their perception, but find out that the majority of the company "sees" itself differently. It is an eye-opening exercise, and one that can help the hiring team better understand the corporate culture, significantly increasing the odds of hiring the right person.

When administering the scorecard, ask respondents to be objective, stressing that there are no "correct" answers. Clarify that a "strong trend" is when your company responds in a specific manner 80 percent of the time.

After collecting the data, note numerical disparities of three points or more—both within and between departments and the company overall. What this means is that if the hiring team ranks the company's approach to decision making a "2" (consensus driven), while people in the department rank that department's approach a "6" (leadership driven), then you need to consider whether that difference indicates a dysfunction. It may or may not. A company that tends toward "innovative" nevertheless may want a finance department that is "steady." If nothing else, this scorecard will bring cultural questions to light for the team to examine.

Since every company has some level of dysfunction, every company needs to factor this into the hiring process. If you have major dysfunction in the department with the open slot, you'll need to decide if you want to hire a change agent to help align the department with the company, or someone who will fit well into the department as it is.

In one recent case I administered this scorecard and found that in the area of teaming, the leadership team scored the corporate culture of the organization as being a 1 (strongly individual) while the rest of the company's average response was an 8 (group oriented). This caused enough consternation to cause the leadership team to suspend the search.

At the client's request I came back in a month and readministered the scorecard. This time the mean and the mode score was a 5—right in the middle of individual and group orientation. Certainly, there is plenty of discussion around this point—did employees consciously (or subconsciously) skew answers in order to "please" management? Would you get similar results in six months? All valid questions, but most importantly this focus on culture allowed the company to get to know itself, resulting in a clearer search and a better hire.

Following is the scorecard. Each area essentially answers the question "What is your company's approach to? . . . "

1.   Decision Making

Guiding question: How are decisions generally made—by consensus or by leadership?

By Consensus   By Leadership

1   2   3   4   5   6   7   8   9   10

2.   Communicating

Guiding question: How do people relate to each other—in a formal and detached way, or in a more informal, personable way?

Formal   Informal

1   2   3   4   5   6   7   8   9   10

3.   Procedures

Guiding question: Do you value consistency of procedures (i.e., are you organized around roles) or flexibility (i.e., are you organized around talents and skills)?

Consistent   Flexible

1   2   3   4   5   6   7   8   9   10

4.   Innovation

Guiding question: Does your company innovate and develop revolutionary products, or does it stick to its core offerings, progressing in steady stages?

Revolutionary   Steady

1   2   3   4   5   6   7   8   9   10

5.   Employee Makeup

Guiding question: Are employees people who seek meaning in their work or are they a resource hired to do what the company wants them to do?

Seek meaning   Resource

1   2   3   4   5   6   7   8   9   10

6. Teaming

Guiding question: Do you reward individuals for what they contribute to groups, or do you reward groups for how they nurture individual development and initiative?

Individuals   Groups

1   2   3   4   5   6   7   8   9   10

7. Winning

Guiding question: Is your company a world of competing rivals, or a world of cooperation and partnerships?

Competitive   Cooperative

1   2   3   4   5   6   7   8   9   10

8. Profits[1]

Guiding question: How much emphasis does your company put on short-term shareholder value versus long-term economic value for all stakeholders?

Short-term   Long-term

1   2   3   4   5   6   7   8   9   10

---

[1]A note to nonprofits—since profitability is not the focus of your organization, you can adapt this profiling tool by replacing the eighth component of culture with the following:

8) Capital resources—Guiding question: How much emphasis does your nonprofit organization put on the direct need for capital versus a non-direct focus on capital?

In other words, is the nonprofit organization one where all employees are asked to concern themselves with the capital necessary to run the organization, or are the nonprofit's capital concerns of no concern to the employees?

If you are interested in a printable version of this document, go to my web site (www.danerling.com) and visit the forms section. You can get there directly through www.danerling.com/content/forms/Cultural%20Scorecard.pdf.

When assessing the scorecards, look carefully at extremes: areas of strong consensus, and areas with a disparity of three points or more. Discuss the results with the hiring team, and keep in mind that the scorecard often says as much about the individual who fills it out as it does about the company and department. Your goal here is not to convince your team members that the culture is one way or another; the goal is to simply note consensus and disparity and ask what the scoring means in terms of the qualities you need for the open position.

Your foundation is set. You now have a base from which you can act. You will revisit this foundation to provide you with direction when making tough decisions. It will keep the process moving consistently and efficiently.

Okay, time to get going! You're now ready to launch the actual hiring process, which begins with preparing your recruiting plan.

MATCH
The Process:
Phase I

Preparing the
Recruiting Plan

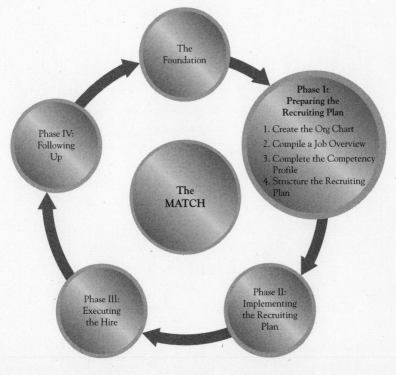

The
Foundation

Phase I:
Preparing the
Recruiting Plan

1. Create the Org Chart
2. Compile a Job Overview
3. Complete the Competency
   Profile
4. Structure the Recruiting
   Plan

Phase IV:
Following
Up

The
MATCH

Phase III:
Executing
the Hire

Phase II:
Implementing
the Recruiting
Plan

Phase I: Preparing the Recruiting Plan begins with the construction of a simple yet surprisingly powerful deliverable—creating the organizational chart. You'll then move into generating the core tasks of developing the job overview and completing the competency profile—both of which are anchored in your mission. You'll finalize this phase by structuring the recruiting plan itself.

Create the Organizational Chart

Step 1

Take my assets, but leave my organization and in five years I'll have it all back.

—Alfred P. Sloan, Jr.

A n organizational chart (or org chart) is the first step in a strong hiring process. Some clients are surprised when I tell them that companies that enjoy success in the art of hiring begin with the organizational chart. Why an org chart, they wonder? For three simple reasons:

1. Creating an org chart forces you to decide exactly **where** the person will fit and what their **title** will be. The org chart provides you with clarity and the grounding you'll need once the interview process starts.

2. The org chart is the "window display" for your position, in the sense that it's meant to give a glimpse of what a store offers—enough to lure the shopper to go inside. In this case, the window shopper is your candidate. Your org chart shows the candidate the level of the position, how many reports the position manages, and to whom he or she reports—all in a single glance. If they like what they see in the org chart, then they'll dive into the job description.

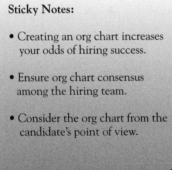

Sticky Notes:

• Creating an org chart increases your odds of hiring success.

• Ensure org chart consensus among the hiring team.

• Consider the org chart from the candidate's point of view.

3. The third reason is a bit less concrete but critical, none-theless. The recruiting documents that you produce form job seekers' first impression of your company. Always assume you're competing with other companies for the interest of your candi-date. Not only do you want the potential employee to under-stand his or her role, but you want them to perceive your company as a structured, highly professional environment. I see the results when I review job descriptions with potential employees. Well written, up-to-date, precisely formatted documents really *do* help shape the candidate's opinion of a company.

There are three basic types of organizational charts: hierar-chical, matrix, and flat. I've found that although the type really doesn't matter, what *does* matter is the symbolic representation of the organization's structure. While it's easy to get caught up in the dialogue around the org chart itself, this is a mistake. It's best to just reflect the structure as it is at the moment, and avoid getting bogged down in details and questions. Remember, all you are doing is trying to develop a sense of your company and an explanation of the current opening.

Here are three organizational charts, followed by a few reflections:

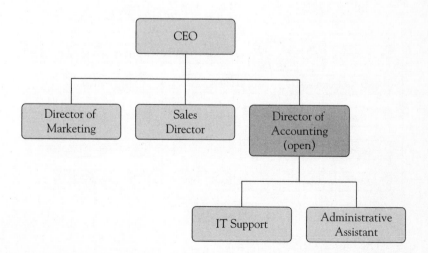

This first org chart is for a small start-up. The CEO had been doing all the accounting in Peachtree software with the help of his administrative assistant. Since sales were going well, he decided to bite the bullet and hire someone to take care of all the accounting/finance, as well as managing the information technology (IT) support role and the administrative assistant.

With a quick glance, you can tell that the right fit would have to be an entrepreneurial individual, capable of relating directly to the CEO. Although this accountant will have a snazzy title, all the daily, mundane tasks are going to fall on his or her desk, so no big egos. You can even correctly surmise that within the company, growth will be dependent on the business plan of the CEO.

This second org chart reflects the accounting and finance department for a fairly small public company. The open position is for a "Director of Financial Operations" who reports to the VP of Accounting, who in turn reports to the chief financial officer (CFO). You can see that this position has some potential for growth, and also that the person in it will have a great deal of supervisional responsibility of both managerial and clerical staff.

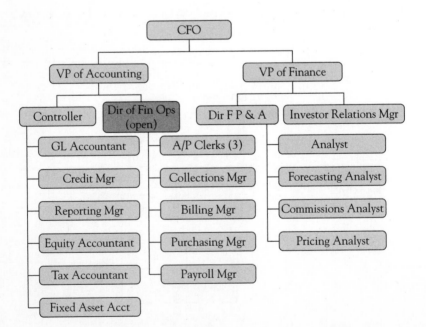

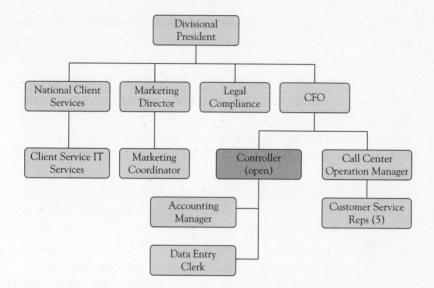

Further, you can glean that a good peer relationship with the controller will be critical to the success of this role.

This third org chart reflects a division of a multibillion-dollar public company. While the company is much larger than the one reflected in the previous org chart, you can immediately see from the diagram that this role has a lesser scope of responsibility. The opportunity to interact and learn from one's peers will clearly not be as available in this case. By simply reviewing this chart a savvy candidate will gain insight into the company and make the first steps in determining their level of interest.

The Deeper Function of an Org Chart

"I don't find org charts very useful," one client confessed to me. "They get in the way of getting work done."

People like my client argue that org charts capture the past instead of focusing on the future, acting to stymie creativity. They rebel against the boxes and lines. Some feel that org charts encourage a narrow view of one's job and, in effect, imply what the employee will *not* do.

Indeed, an org chart should never be a hindrance to action and creative solutions. However, aside from being a powerful sales tool for a potential candidate, the org chart is a *good* thing for your company. Successful companies recognize that an org chart already exists in every organization in *some* fashion—even if it's just in your employees' heads. The very act of putting one on paper is a good test of the company's soundness. All business relationships should be able to be charted. Org charts bring a sense of transparency to the organization and provide a clear picture of responsibilities and reporting relationships—not only up and down, but also across the organization.

An org chart is more than just a page of boxes and lines showing direct and indirect reporting relationships. A business unit—and the business as a whole—has a purpose. An org chart should graphically represent that purpose at a high level. When you look at an org chart of a finance department, for instance, you should be able to trace the path of how the department achieves its goals.

The emphasis on the position's function is very important, especially as smaller businesses begin to grow. Founders of smaller companies can generally manage by their personal styles. But there comes a point where employees have to do the jobs necessary for the business to meet its organizational goals, and not just fit one person's personality and unique skills. This transition can hinder growth and burn out top employees if they don't have a clear sense of their function. The org chart provides them with that clarity, and gives management a tool for growth.

For more sample org charts, visit my web site at www.danerling .com.

Once you have secured an org chart, you can move to the next critical step in the hiring process: compiling the job overview.

6

Compile a Job Overview

Step 2

I hire people brighter than me and then I get out of their way.
—Lee Iacocca

As with steps throughout the MATCH process, the job overview augments the mission of the organization. This is done by clearly tying the functions of the employee with the company's main purpose.

The job overview has two parts:

1. The job description
2. The skills required

Writing the job overview is an exercise in bringing clarity to yourself, your hiring team, and the candidate. Though it may seem like an exercise in writing down the obvious at times, your worst enemy here is the tendency to make *assumptions* about what the role does and the related required skills. Assume nothing. Write it *all* down.

Keep the following formula in mind:

Time spent clarifying a job description + Time spent clarifying skills = Time saved in the long run.

Sticky Notes:

- Set aside two to three hours to compile a job overview.

- The job overview is the job description plus the skills required.

- Skills should be measurable with a clear "yes" or "no."

The job overview should focus on the responsibilities and qualifications necessary for the position. However, you may brush up against some other areas of the overall hiring process—formulating the salary range or marketing the position, for instance. Set those topics aside for the time being; you'll get to them eventually. For now, just stick to the description and the skills.

The Benefits of a Good Job Overview

An intriguing benefit of writing a clear, detailed job overview is that every now and then, you realize you don't actually *need* the position; for you already have someone on staff that can complete the tasks! Assuming you *do* need to hire, however, the job overview:

- Sharpens your own focus on what the job requires
- Forces you to consider the must-haves versus nice-to-haves
- Provides an objective measurement of the candidate
- Provides the basis for a professional training program, if needed
- Helps define the relationship between individuals within a department, as well as between departments
- Provides a basis for evaluation in salary and title
- Allows the candidate to immediately walk in and *know* what their duties are in terms of:
  - First projects
  - Objectives
  - Intended results of this role
- Allows you to clearly evaluate your candidate pool's ability to do the job needed
- Creates a template for future hiring needs in the same area
- Creates a document for return on investment (ROI) and success/ failure review

The Job Description

Most candidates, of course, want to do a good job. Why is it, then, that so many employees wind up as nonperformers? I have found that, in most cases, the issue is simply poor communication, starting with the job description. Employees don't know what to do because no one tells them, or worse yet, someone tells them the wrong thing to work on.

In highly effective organizations, responsibilities and expectations are written down, reviewed carefully, and agreed upon by the new employee and the hiring team. When there is lack of clarity, then both the employer and employee proceed based on their assumptions of the role. If those two sets of assumptions are out of sync, the results can be disastrous. It's sad when an otherwise good employer and good employee clash at review time over a completely avoidable problem. It is therefore imperative to have a well-written job description.

Note that the MATCH process does *not* advocate a job description that details *every move* that an employee makes. In fact, we have found that most effective companies list the desired objectives and hire candidates who are able to use their creativity in achieving those objectives. Top-down, detailed approaches rarely work.

The critical components of the job description are:

- Title of the position
- Department, location, hiring manager, reports to?
- Mission of both the company and the role
- Summary description of role, including key responsibilities
- Percentage of time to be allocated for responsibilities
- Evaluation method for key responsibilities
- Projects to be undertaken
- Percentage of time to be allocated on projects
- Percentage of required time for traveling

Clarifying the Job Description

When the hiring team gets together to write the job description, I suggest starting the dialog by posing the following three questions:

1. What are the three most important objectives this new hire will achieve in their first year and how will they be evaluated on each of those three objectives?

2. After 6 months, where do we expect the new hire to be in the completion of his or her objectives? What about after 3 months? 1 month?
3. Our new hire walks in on their first day: What is their first task? What about the second and third tasks? What comes after that?

Starting with three long-term objectives and working backward, allows the hiring team to focus on the big picture before zooming in on the job description and skills needed for an effective job overview.

The Skills Required

Questions about skills should be answerable with a clear "yes" or "no." In other words, the candidate either possesses them or does not. There isn't much gray area here.

The critical components of this skills arena include:

- Industry knowledge
- Exposure deemed necessary for success (e.g., private equity, venture capital, Wall Street, public company, small company)
- Education
- Accreditations
- Languages spoken
- Software skills
- Number of years deemed critical to success
- Management skills (e.g., people management, hiring and firing, planning, project management)

Be *specific* when you write out the skills. For example, instead of making a general statement like "know Excel," write: "Use pivot tables in Excel to extract data from Oracle to analyze tax data." Make it clear *exactly* what level of exposure your ideal candidate will possess.

Now that you have the job description and the skills required for the role, you combine the two to create a job overview.

Sample Job Overview

Here is a sample job overview that we used successfully. You can find other samples at www.danerling.com.

Accounting Manager–General Ledger (GL) Job Overview

Job description

Position: Accounting Manager–GL
Department: Accounting
Location: Atlanta
Hiring Manager: Controller
Reports to: Controller

Company Mission

To deliver our product to 100 percent of our clients 100 percent of the time in a reliable and personalized manner that allows us to become the clear industry leader in our field.

Job Mission

This position contributes to company success by managing the preparation of consolidated generally accepted accounting principles (GAAP) financial statements, month-end close processes, and alternated account reconciliations.

This position contributes to company success by managing the preparation of consolidated GAAP financial statements, month-end close processes, and all related account reconciliations.

Summary of Key Responsibilities

Responsibilities include but are not limited to the following:
30 percent:
- Prepare monthly, consolidated GAAP financial statements.
- Develop and present monthly financial statement package to include financial results, variance analyses, trends, and actionable recommendations.
- Detail review of balance sheet reconciliations.
- Journal entry review and posting.

30 percent:
- Responsible for month-end close process and working closely with other accounting managers to decrease days in close.
- Develop and implement additional policies and procedures that govern financial statement preparation and monthly close process.

30 percent:
- Interface with auditors (internal and external) on compliance issues and all levels of the organization to communicate financial processes.
- General ledger and new vendor maintenance and review.
- Ensure that all processes and procedures related to execution of general ledger responsibilities are controlled and documented in accordance with the requirements of the Sarbanes-Oxley Act of 2002.

10 percent:
- Lead special projects as required.

Required Skills

1. BS/BA in accounting
2. Full cycle accounting and monthly close experience: 5+ years
3. Experience in financial management practices, including a basic understanding of internal controls sufficient to analyze transactions and activity to determine whether they comply with regulations, terms and conditions, and policies and procedures: 5+ years
4. Securities and Exchange Commission (SEC) reporting experience: 1+ year
5. Public accounting experience: 2+ years
6. Internet service provider experience: 3+ years
7. Certified public accountant (CPA)
8. Comprehensive experience understanding and prior experience with design and implementation of accounting policies and procedures: 5+ years
9. Experience with Microsoft FRx Report Writer: 1+ years
10. International accounting experience: 1+ years
11. Knowledge of Enterprise Resource Planning (ERP) Financials: 3+ years
12. Percentage of travel required: less than 10 percent

Once you've completed the job overview, set it aside for a day and then re-read it—this time looking at it from the candidate's perspective. Put yourself in their shoes. Is the wording clear? Do your requirements seem reasonable—or are you asking for Superman or Superwoman?

Common Mistakes in Job Overviews

1. **Requirements are too inflexible.** I once worked with a company that would not interview a candidate with strong skills in a specific computer-based system (Peoplesoft ERP) because they were looking for experience with a very similar computer system (SAP). The company did not have compelling reasons for this—it was not a subject matter expert role, nor was an implementation on the horizon. In this case, inflexibility led to exceptional talent not being evaluated.
2. **The wording is too vague.** Again, think in terms of *measureable* skills or knowledge. "Good management skills" is vague; "Three years of experience in training new staff" is more precise.
3. **The description is too short.** We have found that writing a long, detailed job overview facilitates a candidate pool that is more likely to be qualified for the job. Longer job overviews seem to lend credibility to the search, enticing the "right fit" and working to turn away the nonqualified candidate.
4. **Lack of care in crafting the description.** Many times, I will review job overviews with poorly organized thoughts, misspelled words, and a poorly formatted structure. In hiring markets, both good and bad, the best organizations always strive to appeal to exceptional talent.

The candidate should be able to visualize the first days on the job and the overall responsibilities and requirements for success. A carefully crafted job overview (job description plus required skills) is your main tool in painting that picture. The effort you put into the job overview will show, and you'll be rewarded not only by making a great first impression but also in setting the stage for a clear and structured interview process.

Create the Competency Profile

Step 3

In determining "the right people," the good-to-great companies placed greater weight on character attributes than on specific educational background, practical skills, specialized knowledge, or work experience.
                                                            —Jim Collins

I n the preceding chapter, we learned that the job overview is designed to focus the hiring team on what the new hire will be doing (the job description), and the skills necessary for success (the required skills). The next step of the MATCH process allows the hiring team to quantify the soft skills necessary to fit into the corporate culture.

The most effective companies recognize that the soft-skill fit is more important than the hard-skill fit. They recognize that hard skills can be taught, but soft skills touch on a basic approach to work—an approach that needs to be consistent with your company's culture and mission. You can't teach these kinds of skills.

The competency profile is the hiring team's tool for getting clear on the soft skills necessary for the job. Unlike the job overview the competency profile measures areas that are harder to quantify. Using the MATCH process will allow your organization to develop an objective and methodical approach for evaluating the competencies of a successful hire.

Sticky Notes:

- The competency profile allows the hiring team to successfully evaluate soft skills.

- No shortcuts.

- Use the "lowest acceptable ranking" to prioritize your search.

The Process

The competency profile is most effective when completed by the prospective new hire's direct manager with follow-up discussion and analysis by the hiring team. A member of the hiring team will need to administer the profile. Shortcuts will short-circuit the complete candidate profile you are trying to establish. Ensure that each competency is carefully evaluated and weighted.

As you will see, in the competency profile we are looking for the "lowest acceptable ranking" on each competency, not the "desired ranking." The difference between these two is critical. Completing the competency profile and indicating "lowest acceptable ranking" allows your hiring team to define the position's most critical soft skills. Just as important, this approach also defines the areas where the candidate need *not* be particularly strong. Prioritizing competencies leads to an efficient and effective interview process.

The title of this book is *MATCH: A Systematic/Sane Approach for Hiring the Right Person Every Time*. The word *sane* weighs heavy in this section. Because we are busy people, I know that we don't have days to evaluate our potential hires across every possible competency. We need to prioritize, and this approach allows us to prioritize on those competencies that *are* critical, thereby injecting sanity into the hiring process.

Over the years I have conducted *thousands* of these profiles—hiring managers almost always "overrank." No matter how carefully the hiring manager tries to focus on "lowest acceptable ranking," they have a hard time resisting the urge to rank every quality a "10." They want it all! However, as you know, there are no perfect employees. Unfortunately, you *can't* have it all. Therefore, the best approach is to review the first 10 competencies (in pencil), and then restart. This technique almost always leads to rankings that are more realistic.

On the following page, I have included the competency profile form, followed by definitions of each competency. You can go to my web site at www.danerling.com and print out a copy for your hiring team.

Competency Profile

With 10 indicating "wildly critical" and 1 indicating "of no importance," indicate the lowest acceptable ranking of each competency
as it relates to the position for which the search is being conducted.

Position: _____

Hiring Manager: _____

Competency Profile Completed by: _____

Competency	Description	Lowest Acceptable Rating
Intellectual		
1. Intelligence	IQ; the ability to think and adapt to a constantly changing world	
2. Logical decision making	Step-by-step processing of information leading to a rational conclusion	
3. Common sense	The skill of making consistent, pragmatic decisions	
4. Creativity	Ability to think "outside of the box" in problem solving	
5. Education	Formal, post–secondary school education	
6. Hands-on training	On-the-job experience	
7. Knowledge of industry trends	Up-to-date knowledge on industry current events	
8. Knowledge of current events	Nonindustry—well read outside of industry	
Communication		
1. Verbal communication	Clearly communicating through speech	

Competency	Description	Lowest Acceptable Rating
2. Written communication	Clearly communicating through writing	
3. Technological communication	Clearly communicating using technology: email, blogs, wikis, PDAs, etc.	
4. Able to run effective meetings	Well planned and orchestrated meetings	
5. Sense of branding	Ability to understand and augment company brand	
6. Image	Conveyance of professionalism in one's image	
7. Listening	Ability to focus on understanding others	
8. Sales focused	Directing business practices to prioritize sales	
9. Capacity to deliver company message	Capable of walking the company line	

Leadership

1. Mission driven	Focuses on the mission of the organization in all business dealings	
2. Executer of corporate vision	Able to take the company where it wants to go	
3. Bottom-line focused	Makes decision based on financial realities	
4. Capable of translating corporate goals to reality	Consistently executes company initiatives	
5. Track record	Past performance	
6. Reputation	The general perceived status of the candidate	

(*Continued*)

(Continued)

Competency	Description	Lowest Acceptable Rating
7. Change agent	Ability to foster change in an organization	
8. Eager to help others succeed	Puts others in front of his/her success	
9. Breeds followership	Leads others	
10. Self-aware	Knows personal strengths and weaknesses	
11. Risk taker	Takes calculated chances	
12. Politically agile	Elegantly gains consensus among people with different views	
13. Capacity for building high-performing teams	Assembles teams who are able to achieve corporate objectives	
14. Integrity	Always does what they say they are going to do	
15. Honesty	Tells the truth	
16. Resourceful	Figures it out no matter how difficult the barrier	
17. Customer focused	Service mentality	

Management

Competency	Description	Lowest Acceptable Rating
1. Strong delegation skills	Gets work done through others	
2. Does not push problems up the organizational chart	Handles problems without assistance from supervisor	
3. Capable of managing to corporate goals	Knows how to utilize a team to hit goals	
4. Strong business acumen	Knowledge of how business works "under the hood"	
5. Can hire and fire	Track record of hiring and firing	

Competency	Description	Lowest Acceptable Rating
6. Can redeploy low performers	Capable of reassigning or demoting those incapable of their work assignment	
7. Can recognize and promote high achievers	Capable of effective management of superstar employees	
8. Maintains a positive work environment	Fosters constructive dialogue and feelings toward the company, coworkers, and the tasks being managed	
9. Manages to individual style	Able to manage teams and individuals based on the given situation	
10. Augments management with technology	Creatively uses technology to manage employees	
11. Provides adequate feedback to team	Shares constructive criticism on a timely basis	
12. Conflict management	Deals with conflict in a direct, positive manner	
13. Maintains a light touch	Rarely do those being managed realize that they are indeed being managed	
14. Comfortable with diversity	Able to effectively work with all types of people	
15. Deadline driven	Works to a clearly set end date	
16. Project management	Effective organization and implementation of group projects	

Personal

1. Passionate	Energized by excellence in the workplace	

(*Continued*)

(Continued)

Competency	Description	Lowest Acceptable Rating
2. Work–life balance	Capable of managing excellence at work and at home	
3. Stress management	Ability to effectively work under pressure	
4. Humorous	Able to effectively use humor in the workplace	
5. Capable of handling constructive criticism	Listens and applies good advice	
6. Commute tolerant	Able to retain sanity while getting to work!	
7. Open to relocation	Capable of moving for the right opportunity	
8. Detail oriented	Crosses all the "t"s	
9. Big picture oriented	Sees the company holistically	
10. Driven toward excellence	Never satisfied with the success of today	
11. Money motivated	Inspired to hit goals that are rewarded monetarily	
12. People motivated	Inspired to hit goals that are rewarded by communal praise or that simply help others	
13. Credential motivated	Inspired to hit goals that are rewarded by job title	
14. Tenacity	Will continue to persist under the most difficult circumstances	
15. Energy	No matter how many times they get knocked down, they jump back up	
16. Organization skills	Structured	

Competency	Description	Lowest Acceptable Rating
17. Independent	Able to make decisions without assistance from management	
18. Track record of personal accomplishment	Shown the ability to accomplish hard-to-reach goals outside of work	
19. Goal driven	Driven by accomplishments	
Other	Ask yourself: are there any other competencies that must be accounted for in terms of this particular position?	

Note: Bradford D. Smart is an author, lecturer, and business consultant on the subject of Topgrading—an assessment methodology using chronological interviews and other best practices.

Some years ago a client introduced me to the concept of evaluating competencies in terms of "lowest acceptable rating," which I incorporated into the MATCH process. Later I found this approach was advocated in the Topgrading process. While I recognize that there can be no claim of ownership in a style of competency profiling, I did want to point out and pay tribute to Mr. Smart's use of this technique.

I've collected these outlined "key competencies" from the thousands of job orders we've taken at my recruiting firm; however, my team periodically reviews and refines the list. While I encourage you to add any competencies that you think will help you evaluate the "right fit" for your specific job, I also challenge you to force-fit my entire list into your evaluation. This is a proven list covering the skills of the modern business professional.

Using the Competency Profile to Prioritize Essential Personality Traits

Once the competency profile has been administered, then the hiring team is charged with ordering the list by ranking—highest to lowest. The 10s are your critical competencies; they go to the top of the list. Suppose that you administered the competency profile and found the highest-ranking competencies to be **common sense, listening, capacity for building high-performing teams,** and **integrity**. Then these are the areas where you spend the greatest amount of time during the interview process.

However, suppose **detail oriented** and **credential motivated** were ranked at the lowest end of the scale—earning 1s. It makes no sense to spend much time (if any) on these competencies. In fact, the benefit of this process is as much in feeling comfortable knowing what you can *avoid* as it is in what you should focus on.

Further, over time you will develop a catalog of competency profiles for your organization. Whenever you profile a corporate executive or an accounts payable clerk, file the data for improvement and reuse. You will soon create a library of competencies that make your organization more efficient and effective.

If the hiring team wishes to reprioritize any item, they should proceed with caution. Part of the strength of the MATCH process is that the search emanates from the direct manager of the new employee. The hiring team should be careful in using its influence to change the priority of any competency.

What about 8s and 9s?

Now what about the 9s? You'll often end up with around four times as many 9s as there are 10s. The 9s are very important to you, too; so you want to explore those. And, geez, the 8s shouldn't be ignored, should they?

The key to "sanely" exploring competencies is to prioritize. List every competency from those ranked 10 to those ranked 1. At that point, the hiring team must decide which competency deserves exploration and which doesn't. The strength of this process is that at least the list has been prioritized. With just a bit of dialogue, the hiring team will be able to move toward interview questions focused heavily on the highest-ranking competencies, to a lesser extent on the lower-ranking competencies, and completely disregarding competencies of no value.

Behavioral Interviewing

From Competency Ratings to Scripted Behavioral Questions

Behavioral interviewing is an interviewing approach based on the belief that previous behavior is the best predictor of future results. In a behavioral interview, the interviewer asks an open-ended question on a key competency and then follows with a series of questions that focus on behavior, responsibility, and results. In addition, by avoiding closed-ended questions (ones that can be answered with a simple "yes" or "no"), the interviewer avoids hypothetical situations that don't demonstrate experience.

For instance, suppose the hiring team recognizes that strong "organization skills" are crucial to a new hire. In a traditional interview, the interviewer may ask the candidate a closed-ended question such as, "Are you organized?" Unless the candidate is completely clueless, they will answer with an enthusiastic "Yes, of course!" Even if the interviewer asks a situational question such as, "How would you handle a department that is currently in need of structure?" it's possible for the candidate to give a compelling answer and never demonstrate they can actually *deliver* the solution. How they *would* do something doesn't mean that they *have* done it or *can* do it.

Keep in mind that behavioral questions unto themselves offer no value. To have value they must work to align the company mission with specific personalities and skills to solve a business problem. If they don't, then a behavioral interview no more effective than a traditional interview. It would be analogous to having a treasure map but no starting point—the treasure map is worthless.

Behavioral interviewing is an important component of the MATCH process. The purpose of behavioral interviewing is to provide an accurate picture of past performance. By scripting interview questions and posing them in the same format with each candidate, an employer is able to evaluate all answers side by side without bias. This "apples to apples" comparison is crucial in terms of one's ability to make the best hiring decisions.

Examples of Behavioral Questions

Behavioral interview questions never "lead the witness." In other words, the type of answer you desire should not be obvious when you ask the question. Below are two examples of nonneutral wording. If you were a candidate who wanted the job, you would know the correct response in both cases:

1. At XYZ Company, we believe that employees must work 60 to 70 hours a week. Do you see yourself being able to adhere to this rigorous schedule?
2. At ABC Company, we don't believe in overtime. Are you the type of person who can get their work done in 40 hours?

Contrast questions 1 and 2 with the following behavioral question:

"Over the past year, on average, how many hours a week did you put in?"

This last question is preferable because it doesn't give the candidate any clues that indicate a desired response. Further, the candidate is being asked about a previous behavior. This approach leads the interviewer to develop a much clearer understanding of the candidate.

Behavioral questions focus on weaknesses as well as strengths. When investigating a candidate's flaws, the interviewer must explore instances where he or she did and did not achieve desired results. While behavioral interviewing is becoming more common, it is still critical to let the candidate know that it is okay to explore weaknesses. The underlying belief of behavioral interviewing is that both companies *and* candidates have limitations.

Below is a script from a behavioral interview. Note the open-ended but targeted questions, as well as the natural, conversational style:

Interviewer: *Tell me about* your organizational style.
Candidate: I am very organized. My desk is meticulously structured. I spend at least 10 minutes at the end of each day ensuring that all my pencils are sharpened and placed in the right place.
Interviewer: Do you have experience managing projects? I'd like to *hear about that*.

Candidate: Oh, absolutely! I managed a system implementation when we integrated a new software package.

Interviewer: Great. Who was on your team?

Candidate: Well, actually, I was reporting to the CIO, but my team consisted of an IT manager, several clerks to enter data, a former controller who really knew the old system, and the IT consulting team.

Interviewer: And *how did you organize* the project?

Candidate: I used Post-it notes to write down all the tasks that each person had to complete on a daily basis. When they got to work, they would read what they had to do that day to make the conversions work.

Interviewer: Did you write Post-it notes for the controller and the IT consulting team?

Candidate: No, they generally worked together while I worked with the IT manager and the clerks.

Interviewer: Did you use any *technological tools* to organize the project?

Candidate: No, but I also kept a notebook in which I recorded daily entries in a very organized fashion.

Interviewer: And *how did the rollout go?* Did you finish the project?

Candidate: They had originally expected it to be done by last November, but now it is dragging on and on. But hey, it wasn't my fault; I even have a quarterly review from the CIO that said my performance was exceptional.

Interviewer: Terrific—but let's go a bit deeper into how you organized the team around the goal. . . .

To help you develop your interview script, I have listed one or two sample behavioral questions for each competency. These questions are intended to be rudimentary guides to be refined and prioritized based on the specifics of your search. The number of behavioral questions appropriate for each competency varies, depending on priority and nature of the hire. For example, I once helped the hiring team script 20 sequential questions based on a single competency. However, in the case of an entry-level position, I suggest three or four questions for the critical competencies.

To clarify: the goal of this profiling process is to clearly define and prioritize the competencies needed to match the right person with the job and the culture of the company. Once you've established these competencies, you align behavioral questions in a logical and time-effective manner.

Competencies	Sample behavioral question(s)
Intellectual	
1. Intelligence—IQ	• Please describe your learning style. • Tell me about the most challenging project you have ever been assigned. How did you adapt? Describe your learning curve.
2. Logical decision making	• How do you process data? • Describe an instance where you collected data to make a decision. What was the result of that decision?
3. Common sense	• Do you describe yourself more as a dreamer or more down to earth? Why?
4. Creativity	• What was the most difficult problem you have faced over the past two years, and how did you overcome it?
5. Education	• How has your formal education aided in your career growth?
6. Hands-on training	• What hands-on training have you found most beneficial to your career development?
7. Knowledge of industry trends	• What industry-specific magazines, periodicals, blogs, and web sites do you keep up with? • What current industry trend do you feel will have the greatest impact on our future?
8. Knowledge of current events—nonindustry	• What are you currently reading for pleasure? • What do you think is the most important issue facing our world today?
Communication	
1. Verbal communication	• Describe your verbal communication style. • If I were to talk to your supervisor, what would they say about your effectiveness as a verbal communicator? How about a peer? A subordinate?

Competencies	Sample behavioral question(s)
2. Written communication	• Describe your written communication style. • If I were to talk to your supervisor, what would they say about your ability to communicate through writing? How about a peer? A subordinate?
3. Technological communication	• What technological tools do you use in your communications? • Give an example where you used technology to achieve a business objective.
4. Able to run effective meetings	• What is your philosophy in terms of business meetings? • How do you ensure that your meetings are achieving the objectives you've set?
5. Sense of branding	• How would you describe your personal brand? • How does your personal brand enhance the company brand?
6. Image	• If we talked to coworkers above, below, and on the same level of the organizational chart as you, how would they describe your image?
7. Listening	• Please describe your listening style. • Give me an example of the last time you failed to listen carefully, and the results that occurred because of that instance.
8. Sales focused	• What is the role of sales in the modern company?
9. Capacity to deliver company message	• When have you been asked to deliver the company message—either internally (departmentally, divisionally, or company-wide) or externally (public speaking, networking event, etc.)? What were the results of your delivery?

Leadership

1. Mission driven	• What is your current company's mission? • How does your current role augment this mission? • Describe your sense of passion for your current company's mission. • What is your personal mission?

(Continued)

(*Continued*)

Competencies	Sample behavioral question(s)
2. Executer of corporate vision	• What concrete actions have you taken in the past year that have helped your current organization to get closer to realizing its vision? • In your opinion, what steps must be taken for an organization to achieve its vision?
3. Bottom-line focused	• How do you measure ROI? • What key metrics do you look at when considering a project's implementation?
4. Capable of translating corporate goals to reality	• What is your track record of goal execution? • Describe a situation where you were unable to deliver on a corporate goal.
5. Track record	• How do you think coworkers above, below, and on the same level on an organizational chart would describe your track record? • What was the low point in your career?
6. Reputation	• Describe your reputation. • When a recruiter calls you, which of your achievements are they most interested in discussing?
7. Change agent	• When have you been brought in to turn an organization (department, company, division, etc.) around? What were the results of your efforts?
8. Eager to help others succeed	• How would people you have supervised and/or managed describe you?
9. Breeds followership	• How do you build consensus on your team?
10. Self-aware	• What is your greatest weakness? If I ask this same question to a reference, do you think they will agree? • What is your greatest strength? If I ask this same question to a reference, do you think they will agree?
11. Risk taker	• What is the greatest risk you have taken over the past year? What were the results of taking that risk?

Competencies	Sample behavioral question(s)
12. Politically agile	• What was the most damaging political faux pas you've made in your career?
13. Capacity for building high-performing teams	• What steps do you take when you have a nonperformer on your team? • What steps do you take when you have a mediocre performer on your team? • What steps do you take when you have a top performer on your team?
14. Integrity	• Describe the last time your integrity was challenged and the outcome of the situation? • Have you ever refused to follow a corporate directive because of ethical concerns?
15. Honesty	• When was the last time you were pressured to be "economical" with the truth, and how did you handle it?
16. Resourcefulness	• Describe an instance where you had to "do more with less." What were your results? • What has been your greatest career accomplishment?
17. Customer focused	• When have you gone above and beyond the call of duty to meet customer needs?
Management	
1. Strong delegation skills	• Describe how you get work done through others.
2. Does not push problems up the organizational chart	• When is the last time you had to go up the organizational chart in order to find a solution to a problem?
3. Capable of managing to corporate goals	• What business initiatives were you responsible for during the past year? • How was your performance evaluated in terms of these initiatives?

(Continued)

(*Continued*)

Competencies	Sample behavioral question(s)
4. Strong business acumen	• If I were to talk to the leadership team at your current company, what areas of your general business knowledge would they indicate need improvement? In what areas of general business knowledge would they indicate your greatest strength lies?
5. Can hire and fire	• Tell me the story of the toughest situation where you had to let someone go.
6. Can redeploy low performers	• Tell me a success story where you reformatted an employee's job description so they were able to be successful at a less demanding job.
7. Can recognize and promote high achievers	• Describe your track record with high achievers
8. Maintains a positive work environment	• How would your peers—those above and below you on the organizational chart—describe your ability to create a positive work environment under any circumstances?
9. Manages to individual style	• How do you adapt your management style to accommodate different personality types?
10. Augments management with technology	• How do you use technology in achieving your management goals?
11. Provides adequate feedback to team	• How would your peers—those above and below you on the organizational chart—describe your ability to provide constructive feedback?
12. Conflict management	• What has been the toughest conflict you have had to mediate over the past year, and what was the outcome?
13. Maintains a light touch	• How do you get others to do what you want them to do without feeling that you are forcing their hand?

Competencies	Sample behavioral question(s)
14. Comfortable with diversity	• What does it mean to you to have a commitment to diversity? • Describe a time where you misread a cultural difference and it led to unexpected consequences.
15. Deadline driven	• What is the last deadline that you missed and why did you miss it?
16. Project management	• What are the steps of managing a project from start to finish?

Personal

1. Passionate	• What do you love about your current job? • What was your proudest career moment?
2. Work-life balance	• On average, how many hours did you work per week over the past year? • Describe your most satisfying activity outside of work.
3. Stress management	• When is the last time you allowed stress to cloud your judgment? • How do you constructively deal with stress?
4. Humorous	• Describe an instance where you used humour at work to diffuse a tense situation or build comradery on your team.
5. Capable of handling constructive criticism	• Have you ever been criticized (either formally or informally) when you thought that the reviewer was incorrect? What was your specific reaction? • Describe a time when you received a great deal of constructive criticism. How did you react?
6. Commute tolerant	• How much time have you spent over the past year commuting on a daily basis?
7. Open to relocation	• Under what circumstances would you consider relocating?
8. Detail oriented	• When has your focus on "dotting I's and crossing T's" positively affected the company's bottom line?

(Continued)

(*Continued*)

Competencies	Sample behavioral question(s)
9. Big-picture oriented	• When has your focus on seeing the big picture positively affected the company's bottom line?
10. Driven toward excellence	• Describe a time where either you personally or your team achieved a goal against all odds.
11. Money motivated	• When has money been a principle motivator for you to go above and beyond your responsibilities?
12. People motivated	• When have people been a principal motivator for your going above and beyond your responsibilities?
13. Credential motivated	• When have you gone above and beyond for an improvement in title?
14. Tenacity	• What is the most challenging business objective you have ever achieved?
15. Energy	• How do you maintain a high energy level at all times?
16. Organization skills	• Tell me about your organizational style.
17. Independent	• How do you like to be managed?
18. Track record of personal accomplishment	• Outside of work, what is the toughest accomplishment you've ever achieved?
19. Goal driven	• What goals did you set for yourself last year? • Which goals did you achieve, and which did you miss?

Prior to speaking with candidates, the interview scripting process should be undertaken by key members of the hiring team. The competency profile should be organized, with the "10s" receiving first billing in your interview script. By working down the list of prioritized competencies, you ensure that you are managing your interview time most effectively.

Common Questions

What about psychological assessments?

Used correctly, psychological assessments can offer great value in the hiring process. From short pencil-and-paper tests, to extravagant computerized profiles, to time spent with a corporate psychologist, assessments are designed to predict success within the workplace as well as determining effective coaching and management techniques.

Some organizations wisely use this information in hiring decisions. Others do not. The bottom line is: companies that allow psychological assessments to dominate their hiring decisions are not as successful as those that complement their hiring process with these tools.

How much of the soft skills do we advertise?

What do you think would happen if you wrote in the job overview, "Looking for an entrepreneurial personality type"? I guarantee every candidate you interviewed would have a prepared answer highlighting their entrepreneurial spirit. No, you don't want to show your hand completely.

However, there are times where you *do* need to use certain wording to entice the right people. The best approach is to use that competency wording (e.g., entrepreneurial . . . family environment . . . fast moving . . .) in the section of the job overview that describes your *company*. Candidates with similar traits will be naturally drawn to your company.

How does an organization attract a superstar in a changing or dysfunctional environment?

Several years ago, I had the opportunity to assist a hiring team in a search for a controller immediately following an acquisition. The acquired company's financials were a mess! The chief financial officer (CFO) estimated that it would take the controller at least six months of 70+-hour workweeks to get things back in order. The hiring team was concerned that a superstar would not be interested in a role that initially required so much clean-up work.

Instead of trying to "smooth over" the brutal facts—the general ledger was a mess, there was a ton of work to do, all the responsibility was going to fall on shoulders of the controller—I advised that we play up the job's difficulties. We didn't put the ugly details in the small print; instead, we advertised the positive aspects of the difficultly in the initial phases of the job. Our job title became "controller needed to navigate a difficult acquisition."

By clearly outlining the role's challenges, we were able to attract a candidate who thrived in the role. The new controller knew exactly what she was getting into and saw the position as an opportunity to prove herself. Further, there was no confusion regarding the initial overtime; the expectations had been clear in this regard since the onset of the interview process.

Through this experience and others like it, I have come to recognize that just as there are people who love extreme sports, there are people who love extreme career challenges. Tons of overtime and the job of cleaning up a major mess was not a negative to the new controller, but rather an exciting challenge.

As an interesting aside, after a year of hard work the controller did start to see the light at the end of the tunnel. She called me one day to tell me that she was going to take a two-week vacation. Things were under control; she was leaving the office before dark, playing tennis on the weekend, and even taking a class in pottery. I'd like to say that she began to enjoy her life of leisure, but the truth is she soon quit her job to go clean up another mess for another company. She had become bored—incapable of being satisfied once systems were in place.

No bones about it—creating the competency profile is a major effort of brainstorming and heavy lifting for you and the hiring team. Whereas creating the job overview is often an exercise in gathering and clarifying information that's already there, creating the competency profile forces you to think deeply about the values that complement your company's mission and culture, and then wrestle all of that into some kind of scripted form. So congratulate yourself on making it through this part. Well done.

Now, on to the plan.

CHAPTER 8

Structure the Recruiting Plan

Step 4

If you think hiring professionals is expensive, try hiring amateurs.
—Anonymous

N ow that we've systematically documented the org chart, the job overview, and the competency profile—the elements of the process that will help define "who" and "what" you're looking for—it's time to consider the recruiting plan—the part that gives you the "how" and "when."

A structured recruiting plan will make your hiring efforts more efficient by allowing you to focus resources on areas that provide the greatest results. Instead of a scattershot approach, the recruiting plan should be designed to ensure that the right people are aware of the job for which you are hiring. The plan's goal is to make available a pool of qualified candidates at the salary range that the organization has budgeted. Ideally, each potential employee should be qualified for the job, thereby allowing the hiring team to make a "best fit" decision.

Many companies utilize only a single source for their recruiting activity. For example, consider a typical hiring effort. The organization runs an ad on a job board, to which a multitude of candidates respond. The hiring manager reviews the résumés, or perhaps even

Sticky Notes:

- The goal of the recruiting plan is to provide a pool of candidates capable of doing the job.

- Consider the advantages/ disadvantages of someone already employed.

- Utilize ordinary and out-of-the ordinary ways of finding employees.

utilizes résumé-scanning software searching for key words. A total of three candidates out of the stack of hundreds are asked to come in for an interview based on industry experience, software, salary, and previous positions held. An offer goes to the best candidate of the three, and the others are discarded.

In my experience, this is the recruiting plan for many companies. Though it works on occasion, most of the time, it does not.

There are numerous problems with this system. For one, while job boards are terrific recruiting tools, in order to be effective in this scenario, the candidate must be *actively seeking employment*. Second, based on the 10 years I've spent watching the hiring process, hiring based on skills alone is almost always a mistake. As we covered in depth in previous chapters, hiring the right "fit" for an organization is infinitely more important than hiring the right "skill set." Skills can be taught; attitude cannot. Third, a single candidate source rarely allows a hiring manager to objectively analyze the talent market by comparing and contrasting all available candidates.

Another oft-repeated mistake is to hire based on recommendation. I have personally made this error several times. Here is how it went for me: I had an open position, and a candidate came highly recommended from a trusted source—in my case it was a relative, but it could have just as easily been a coworker, friend, or business partner. Instead of remaining objective, I became emotional. I let my relationship with the trusted source sway my thinking. I decided to cut short the interview process since someone I know and trust had spoken so highly about this person. I wound up hiring a dud. The only good news is that I learned a lesson and now follow my own advice: stick to an objective process.

Final Check before Launch of Recruiting Plan

Before the hiring team acts upon the recruiting plan, I believe that it is critical to ask the following questions:

1. Can you solve the problem **internally?** Is there any out-of-the-box thinking that will get the job done?

2. Can this role be handled by **outsourcing**, or by using a **contractor?**
3. What is the **impact** on the company if the position goes unfilled?
4. Is the **timing** right? Is there another position that should be filled first? (For example, do you need to hire a manager first, so that he or she can have input to hiring for the rest of the department?)
5. Who is **currently fulfilling the responsibilities** of the role?
6. One more time—is it **absolutely essential** to the organization's mission that you make this hire?

Questions You Need to Ask Your Team

If the hiring team determines that it is time to make the hire, then it's time to execute a recruiting plan. Here are 10 questions to ask in constructing the recruiting plan:

1. What size company does your ideal candidate come from? Does it matter if he/she has divisional responsibility within a larger organization?
2. Is there an industry (or industries) from which you want to recruit?
3. Are you willing to relocate the ideal candidate?
4. What is the budget for the recruiting effort?
5. Is there a specific individual who can be identified and recruited? What are the political ramifications of recruiting that individual? Can your company go directly after that individual, or should you hire a recruiter?
6. What is the salary range for this role? Will the salary range you've identified allow you to compete for top talent?
7. Will you use a recruiter, or do you have the internal resources that will be able to find the right candidate?
8. What resources will you use to pursue this candidate? Some potential resources include:
   - The Internet
     - Job boards
     - Blogs
     - Company web site
     - Advertisements on web sites
     - Social networking sites

- Other media, including:
  - Newspaper
  - Magazines
  - Billboards
  - Flyers
- Incentivized employee referrals
- Bulk email or direct mail—you can buy lists of almost any demographic (I leave it to you to ensure that you are sticking to anti-spam regulations)
- Contract recruiting—bringing in an hourly contract recruiter to assist human resources (HR) with the execution of the recruiting plan
- Sponsorship of professional organizations and conventions that would be attended by your ideal candidate
- Sponsored events—free food and drink are great ways to entice potential candidates to come learn more about your company
- Job fairs
- Hiring a contingency or retained search firm

9. How are you going to attract the attention of your ideal candidate?
10. Are you searching for a candidate who is working or not working? (Note the next section for advantages and disadvantages of recruiting currently employed candidates)

The Advantages/Disadvantages of Hiring an Employed Candidate

Advantages	Disadvantages
Current proven track record (since the candidate is currently employed, you can be more certain that they are high quality).	Plenty of companies retain marginally performing candidates regardless of the quality of their work.
Sends a positive message to employees (we are such an attractive place to work that folks are leaving our competition to join our company; OR, we are such an attractive place that folks are willing to switch industries to join our company).	Salary requirements may be as much as one third higher than market in order to lure the candidate to the new organization.

(Continued)

(Continued)

Advantages	Disadvantages
Provides the ability to address specific need within the company—for instance, if a public company needs improvement in their SEC reporting process, then finding a proven 10K/10Q expert who is currently successful in another organization is oftentimes a successful strategy.	Legal issues such as noncompetes and trade secrets.
Reduces training expense, since you are hiring a proven commodity.	May cause bad blood between companies—will your recruiting efforts lead to a talent war?
	Harder to check references.
Allows you to help others grow their careers; some companies purposely set growth criteria too high, thereby forcing people to stagnate in roles; others don't have room for upward mobility; and others still are not structured well enough to afford growth for talented individuals. Sometimes it takes a change in environment in order for a person to grow, and helping someone reach their career aspirations is a rewarding experience. By celebrating this philosophy of growth, you are able to instill a very positive work environment.	
Initial excitement from the candidate can be a positive boost for a department and teams as well (there's an almost certain guarantee of intense productivity from the candidate for the first six months since they will feel a need to prove themselves).	Some folks want to change companies for the wrong reasons—money alone, or the inability to manage office politics.

Advantages	Disadvantages
By hiring employed candidates, you can be sure that the individual is genuinely interested in the opportunity, and is not just a "tire kicker" or someone who just needs a job—whatever that job might be.	Employed candidates are harder to both locate and recruit. It can be an exhausting process, and at the end of the day, they still may decline the offer. Remember, making a career change is a frightening event. It can be very easy for a candidate to lose the desire to make a change, even for an opportunity that seems ideal to an outsider.

Common Recruiting Methods

As mentioned earlier, there are a variety of recruiting methods available to employers today. The methods selected for any given position will be those that reach the greatest number of candidates with the experience, training, and skills needed in that position. Following are some of the more common strategies.

Media Sources

Media sources include advertisements in newspapers and magazines, on radio, and on television. Newspaper advertisements can reach a large number of qualified candidates for entry-level and unskilled jobs—a group from which employers can then select the best-qualified candidate. Professional journals reach candidates who stay current in their fields of practice. Radio and television ads, although expensive, can provide candidates when employers need to fill a large number of jobs quickly.

Internet Job Boards

For many white-collar job seekers, job boards provide access to a large number of positions throughout the country. This can be a cost-effective way for employers to reach a wide audience. The drawback is that they often result in a large number of applicants that don't possess the qualifications for the job being advertised. This large pool can make it very time consuming to find qualified candidates.

State Employment Offices

Each state has an agency that provides some type of job search assistance to those who are unemployed. Employers are usually able to list open jobs with these agencies for little or no cost.

Company Web Sites

Most corporate, government, and nonprofit web sites have an "employment" or "careers" page on which current openings are listed. In most cases, interested candidates can complete applications online.

Colleges and Universities

Employers who are seeking candidates for management training programs or entry-level professional positions can often recruit graduating seniors through colleges' and universities' employment offices.

Job Fairs

A job fair allows employers to see a large number of candidates at a single time.

Alumni Employees

Call up past employees. Ask them to consider coming back. Even if they say "no," rely on their loyalty for high-quality candidate referrals.

Previous Applicants

Sometimes the recruiting plan produces several highly qualified candidates for an opening. Many effective organizations maintain contact with the qualified candidates who were not selected to have them on tap when other openings become available.

Retained Search Firm

A retained search firm is paid a fee to conduct a search, which the employer must pay in full whether or not a candidate is hired.

Contingency Search Firm

Agencies that perform contingency searches submit candidates to employers for consideration; if an employer hires the candidate, the agency receives a fee.

Social Networking Sites

Social networking is here to stay, and it is clearly the best recruiting tool that has been introduced during my tenure in the business. Social networking strategies include targeted marketing campaigns, job postings, and sourcing techniques.

Out-of-the-Ordinary Ways of Recruiting

To shake up your thinking around the best approach to finding a candidate, consider the following alternatives to the standard recruiting strategies:

- Call up a candidate who rejected your offer in the past three to six months. If they made a mistake going somewhere else, then (a) they probably realize it by now, and (b) they're too embarrassed to come back to you and admit it. Your call might stimulate positive discussions on revisiting the opportunity to join the team. Even if they don't leave their current position, they'll be flattered by your interest, keep you in mind for the future, and may even recommend someone to you.

- Review references from past candidates. In fact, whenever you speak with references on a candidate's behalf, make notes of your impressions of that particular reference—in addition to what they say about the candidate. Use these notes later on in your recruiting efforts.
- Talk with outside salespeople and your vendors. This group is already motivated to bring you value, and if they are good at their jobs, they will know a great deal about your culture. Some might even work with your competitors.
- Keep tabs on your competitors' layoffs. This tactic can be tricky because companies will, obviously, try to hang on to their best people.

During my tenure in recruiting, I have observed some wildly creative methods of recruiting. For example, a technology company did a focused mailing to a group of identified candidates. The mailing consisted of a glossy marketing piece detailing the company and its culture, along with an attractively packaged iPod containing a recorded recruiting message from the CEO. This approach succeeded in generating great interest from the identified talent pool.

Whatever the recruiting approach, it must align with the organization's culture. If the recruiting effort is incongruent to the culture, the process will produce the wrong candidates. For example, a conservative law firm wouldn't achieve desired results by employing scantily clad women to pass out flyers at the local watering hole, just as the creative marketing firm shouldn't send out a conservatively written three-page letter highlighting the long-term growth of the organization.

No matter what approach you take, documentation must be kept and analyzed so you can figure out what works and repeat that activity. I know of one company that runs recruiting ads in several different mediums, and each ad has a different phone number. The company tracks the calls and analyzes the individual ads' success. If one of the sources is underperforming, they change the format or, in some cases, drop coverage altogether. While this level of complexity may be impossible for some firms, constant feedback is necessary in the recruiting plan.

Finally, no matter what the approach, the key to recruiting is consistent effort. Many companies complain to me about lack of talent; yet when I ask about their recruiting plan, they either don't have one, or have relegated duties to a clerical person whose desk is already filled with multiple projects.

The best companies make recruiting a top priority, one that's supported from the top of the organization. Corporations filled with exceptional talent are in the habit of putting people first—no exceptions. Great companies are always recruiting.

Never Set Hiring Deadlines

We have a remarkable client with a near-perfect track record for hiring decisions. Her favorite quote is "never settle." Her sense of leadership has resulted in a department who chants the "never settle" mantra whenever they are given the opportunity to hire. As such, their results are nothing less than spectacular.

I once observed her team under great pressure to hit quarterly deadlines. They needed a reporting specialist in the worst way. But the team worked together to cover the hole in the department. Their refusal to "settle" meant that they absolutely would not make a band-aid hire.

Because they consistently adhere to this rule, her team has banded into an incredibly cohesive unit. Each person in the department looks at themselves as special and elite, carrying a notable sense of pride in their work. They never seemed to be impatient to make the right hire because they recognize the value of waiting for the right person.

The philosophy of "never settle" consistently provides extraordinary results, and exemplifies why it is never a good idea to set a hiring deadline. A company should never force a hire just to "get a warm body in there." It's far better to come up with an alternative solution for getting the work done than it is to hurt the organization in the long term with a mishire.

Thoughts on Recruiting Firms

There are many terrific recruiting firms and recruiters out there. Unfortunately, there are also many who focus too much on short-term financial gains with little to no consideration for candidates or clients. There is a tendency for the business community to allow the bottom of the barrel to set the bar for the rest of the recruiting community—and that is really too bad.

There have been instances in which my company has been called upon to do a search, only to find that there are 10 other firms involved in that very search. Instead of looking at the recruiter as a business partner, some companies attempt to classify the service as a commodity. The drawback of this approach is that the truly professional recruiter winds up passing on the search, and the company winds up with the same mediocre level of recruiting service. And so the recruiting perception is perpetuated.

My advice when using a recruiting firm is to develop a relationship long before a search is even needed. Learn about styles and specialties, and then when the right search comes along, give the recruiting firm the opportunity to act as a trusted advisor.

MATCH

The Process:
Phase II

Implementing
the
Recruiting Plan

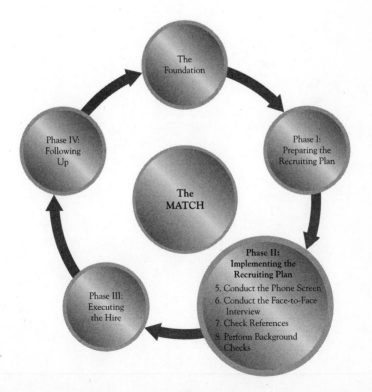

Famous boxer Mike Tyson used to say, "Every boxer has a plan—until they get hit." Though you needn't fear being knocked unconscious by the hiring process, you *do* need to recognize that much of what happens as you **implement the recruiting plan** threatens to knock you off course. For one, the pace of action can put pressure on you to cut corners as you conduct phone screens and then face-to-face interviews. You will also be engaging in quality control by conducting reference checks and completing background checks. Keeping the hiring team coordinated and following a consistent process is a continuing challenge. And the candidates themselves—in their eagerness to highlight their best qualities—will test your ability to stay focused on finding out all the information you need to know for your decision. This phase is the most demanding, so make absolutely sure that you're sticking to the plan.

9

Conduct the Phone Screen

Step 5

I . . . apply the '4-E (And 1-P) Framework' for hiring that I've found consistently effective, year after year, across businesses and borders. The first E is positive energy. It means the ability to go go go—to thrive on action and relish change. The second E is the ability to energize others, and inspire them to take on the impossible. The third is edge, the courage to make tough yes-or-no decisions. The fourth E is execute—the ability to get the job done. Then I look for that final P, passion—a heartfelt, deep and authentic excitement about work.

—Jack Welch

Phone Screen

The objective of the phone screen is to determine if you should continue the interview process with the candidate. You'll make this determination by deciding, at the 30,000-foot level, if his or her skills, personality, and goals match your organization's needs. Used correctly, the phone screen will increase your recruiting plan's efficiency by quickly narrowing your candidate pool by 50 percent.

Because you have developed a job description that details the ideal candidate's skills and personality traits, you should be able to quickly review the résumés and cover letters you've received, and make a reasonable first cut. Skills are easier to evaluate on paper than are personality traits, which is fine. You're not expected to be 100 percent certain of every aspect of the candidate at this point; that's what the phone screen and the rest of the interview process is for.

As we have stressed previously, the hiring manager should be involved in

Sticky Notes:

- Use the phone screen to narrow your candidate pool by 50 percent.

- Maintain consistency from call to call by utilizing a script.

- Use the job overview to specify "knockout" and "go forward" points.

as many steps of the interview process as possible. The phone screen is the first personal contact a candidate will have with an organization, and the sooner you can start building rapport, the better. However, depending on your company's size, the position being hired, and the workload—the administrator or the recruiter from the hiring team may need to handle the phone screen. If that is the case, then the hiring manager must, at a minimum, assist in driving the content of the phone screen script that the hiring team creates.

Developing and Using a Telephone Screening Form

When you're hiring for a specific position, you should use the same set of phone screen questions with every candidate. This approach ensures that you get all of the information you need from every applicant. Remember, a successful hiring process hinges on gathering as much of an apples-to-apples comparison as possible among candidates. Consistency and thoroughness are paramount.

I strongly suggest a position-specific telephone interview form. The good news is that once you develop the form, you can reuse it every time you need to refill the position until the basic requirements change. At that point, any updating you do is simply a matter of making a few tweaks to the form, rather than rebuilding it from scratch.

There is no "magic number" of questions to ask during a telephone screening interview. To determine what questions should be on your form, the hiring team should start with the job overview. The hiring team can create "knockout" points that automatically disqualify a candidate. For example:

Knockout Point: Candidates who do not have _____ (specific knowledge/skill/experience/competency; for example, Microsoft Excel formulas) do not meet the **basic** requirements for the position and are therefore not to be considered as potential candidates for the position.

On the flip side, I suggest setting criteria for a "go forward" that allows the phone screener—regardless of his or her level—to invite a candidate for an interview. For instance, if the screener discovers that a candidate has a satisfactory mastery of four skills deemed critical for the position, then that would be a green light for a face-to-face interview. The advantage of this technique is that it allows the person conducting the phone screen to avoid the need to consult with the hiring team.

Most organizations conduct a one-on-one telephone screening. However, there are other approaches. The most common alternate is to have a second person listen in on or participate in the telephone screening interview and rate the candidate as well. The two interviewers then compare notes and make a joint recommendation on whether to pursue a candidate. Organizations that utilize this approach find that the cost of having two people on the call is outweighed by a decrease in mishires.

Before we move forward, let's briefly cover discrimination. Not only is it morally and ethically wrong to discriminate based on criteria other than a candidate's ability to do the job, it is also bad business. Discriminating based on race, color, religion, sex, national origin, disability, or age is a federal offense in the United States.

The Dos and Don'ts of Interviewing

Effective interviewing is an art brimming with complex psychological issues. Unfortunately, our litigious society only serves to further complicate the interview process. To effectively navigate the legal tightrope, interviewers must limit inquiries to job-related issues *only*. It is imperative during the interview process to avoid questions concerning race, creed, color, religion, national origin, age, sex, disability, or veteran status. Improper questions made during the interview process—even if asked innocently and without intention to discriminate—will lead to legal hot water.

Here are several sample interview questions that further elucidate what is inacceptable and acceptable:

Inappropriate Interview Questions

- What is the nationality of your parents or spouse?
- What religious holidays do you observe?
- Do you plan to marry?
- Do you plan to have children?
- Did you ever have any other names from the one you are using now?

Appropriate Interview Questions (as long as they are job-related)

- Are you eligible to work in the United States?
- What foreign languages do you speak?
- Are there any other names under which your employment may be verified?
- Do you have any family, business, or social obligations that would prevent you from working consistently or overtime or prevent you from traveling?

Never stray from questions that are directly related to a person's ability to do the job. And when in doubt, don't ask. If you feel that there is an area you need to question, but are unsure of the legality, check with your legal team and ask on the second interview. By keeping this in mind, an interviewer will be able to move beyond legal concerns and focus on the candidate's ability to be successful in the position.

Tips on the Phone Screen

- **Keep the call short.** Your calls should take around 15 minutes, and shouldn't exceed 30 minutes. Remember, the point is to figure out if the candidate meets enough of the requirements to warrant a face-to-face interview.
- **Don't discuss the specifics of the job requirements.** Keep in mind that if this individual passes the screening, they will be coming in for an interview. There is no value in thoroughly exploring the candidate's skills during this stage of the process. Your objective is merely to get a snapshot.

- **Be consistent from one call to another.** You are a professional representing your organization. Whether it is the first or the hundredth call of the day, you owe it to your company and the candidate on the other side of the phone to be enthusiastic and upbeat. At the same time, do not oversell. The goal is simply to ascertain if it makes sense to have this person come in.
- **Script your calls.** Take time with the hiring team to formulate a complete script. Start with an overview of the company and the role for which the candidate is being considered; then move into a list of questions regarding his or her ability to perform the job. Compile the responses of the candidates for future review.

Conducting the Actual Phone Screen

Setting the right tone is important when conducting your actual phone screen. **We find this format works best:**

1. Clarify the purpose of the call.
2. Provide a two-minute summary of the company and the reason behind the search.
3. Ask scripted behavioral questions that have been supplied by the hiring team.
4. Clarify and close.

Always be prepared to take notes. Doing this while keeping up a conversation is challenging, but it is absolutely necessary to ensure that you have this information. Leave five minutes open after the conversation to fill in the details and your impressions. Save your computerized notes in a place where the hiring team can review and add to them at a later date.

Sample Phone Screen Questions

The phone screen process should allow you to identify candidates who possess the requisite job skills and traits that align with your company culture. Following are examples of effective phone screen inquiries:

1. Describe your management style.
2. How do you utilize pivot tables in your current role as tax manager?
3. Give an example of a time where you were charged with reducing days sales outstanding (DSO). What specific actions did you take, and what were the results?

Note that each of these three questions are open-ended and focus on a very specific job requirement (question 1 focused on management; question 2 focused on a specific Excel skill; question 3 focused on experience on an explicit accounting management function).

Now, contrast these three questions with the following "traditional" phone screen questions:

1. How many people do you manage?
2. Do you have experience with pivot tables?
3. We currently have a problem with our DSO. Do you have experience in this area?

Closing and Clarification

There are three potential outcomes at the conclusion of a phone screen:

1. The candidate is top tier and therefore scheduled for a face-to-face interview.
2. The candidate is put in the pending file, meaning that they're a possibility, just not a first-round possibility. If no first tier candidates are hired, you will review this file and consider bringing in this person.

3. The candidate is identified as not a fit for this particular position. Their information should be filed for future opportunities in a different area.

Following are closing scripts for each of these outcomes:

For candidates who meet the requirements for a face-to-face interview:

"Mike, I sincerely appreciate your time today. Judging from your résumé and our short discussion, I believe that you are qualified for the job. If you remain interested, I'd like to invite you to thoroughly discuss the opportunity with the hiring manager. During that interview, you will be asked many more probing questions about your skills and competencies. This interview will last roughly two hours. If that goes well, the next steps in the process would be for us to complete reference checks and appropriate background checks. There will be a team interview, and a final dinner with the hiring manager. Our interview process is thorough so that we can ensure that our new hires are successful. The hiring manager can interview you on _____. I will follow up with you by sending you a copy of our data sheet and a confirmation of your interview time. Please complete the datasheet before arriving, including your salary history and complete set of references. On the day of your interview, please call to confirm your appointment. Do you have any questions before we conclude?"

For candidates in the pending category:

"Mike, I sincerely appreciate your time today. You certainly have an impressive track record. We are currently interviewing a number of candidates for this role, and at this stage of the process I would like to file your résumé for future review. Over the next two weeks we will be reevaluating your file. Should you not hear back from us, then I would suggest you look at other opportunities. In either case, we wish you the best and look forward to further discussions."

For candidates who do not show the skills necessary to warrant a face-to-face interview:

"Mike, I sincerely appreciate your time today. You certainly have an impressive track record. We are currently interviewing a number of candidates for this role, and at this stage of the process I would like to file your résumé for future review. Should we wish to ask you in for an interview, either for this or any other opportunity, we will give you a call. In the meantime, I suggest you look at other opportunities, and we wish you the best in your endeavors."

Recently, I shared this script with a friend and business associate that found it to be disingenuous in that we never said "no." I understood his point, but I still stand by the script for two reasons. First, just because the candidate was not a fit for this specific job, he or she might indeed be ideal for another. So, in fact, we are being genuine. Second, it is polite. We don't slam the door in the candidate's face, but we do encourage the candidate to look elsewhere.

Time-Saving Tips for Phone Screens

Trying to coordinate phone screens with numerous candidates can be extremely time consuming. Instead of scheduling each candidate, try issuing a general email to each of the potential candidates using the following format:

Dear _____,

Thanks for your interest in this position. I would be delighted to talk to you about your career goals, and how they match with this opportunity.

Please give me a call any day this week between the hours of 4:00 to 5:30. Schedule roughly 15 minutes for us to talk.

Based on our discussion, we will determine whether it makes sense to continue the conversation.

Thanks again for your interest.

This approach is effective, because it puts the responsibility for time management on the potential candidates. It also helps to alleviate "tire kickers" by requiring that the candidates take action. You are quickly able to determine if this individual is truly interested—as well as capable of following directions.

The approach does require that you are at your desk during the hours you indicate, and in some cases, you will be swamped with calls. In my opinion, this is a positive, because you are able to compress your communications by having one candidate hold while you finish a call with another. Sometimes you will be overwhelmed, but I have found that to happen very infrequently. (Note that I purposely schedule these calls for the end of the day, using the end of business hours to more effectively manage my time.)

Alternatively, use e-mail scheduling software to manage your time with each candidate. Once confirmed, use the candidate's ability to call on time as a "knockout point." If they miss the call, don't go out of your way to reschedule the appointment.

There are times, however, when neither approach is appropriate— for example, when hiring an executive, or an information technology (IT) role in high demand. But there *are* many instances in which this method will allow you to more effectively manage your time.

Using the Proper Equipment

It's best to avoid conducting the telephone screen over a cell phone. While this may seem like common sense to you, it's not to everyone. A friend of mine who was a candidate for a director-level position recently suffered through a telephone screening interview conducted over a recruiter's cell phone. The reception was so poor that he could hear only about half of what the recruiter was saying, and kept having to ask to repeat or clarify what she was asking. After a few minutes, my friend suggested that the interview be rescheduled for another time; the recruiter said, "That's okay. I can hear you just fine."

The moral of the story: it is important not only that you be able to clearly hear and understand the candidate, but that the candidate is able to clearly hear and understand *you*. When you couple this problem with the dropped signals that can also plague cell phone interviews, you end up with a telephone screening interview that has so completely disrupted the interview process that it is practically worthless.

Thoughts on Recruiting Firms and the Screening Process

Despite how outrageous this story sounds, I assure you it is true. A hiring manager once called me because he had just fired the recruiting firm he engaged on a search. After spending nearly an hour describing his criteria for hiring a new controller, the manager was surprised to get an email from the recruiter just hours after their initial call. He opened the email—and found 42 résumés attached!

A lot of people know that when you're making spaghetti, you can tell if the noodles are done by throwing them against the wall to see if they stick. While this might be an acceptable approach in a kitchen, it is not an acceptable approach to hiring.

If you've engaged an effective recruiting firm, the high-level sorting-out process should absolutely be done already. You should expect that any candidate from a reputable firm will be thoroughly interviewed by your recruiter. Good recruiters should send only qualified candidates, which allows you to skip the phone screen process.

10

Conduct the Face-to-Face Interview

Step 6

There is something that is much more scarce, something finer far, something rather than ability. It is the ability to recogonize ability.
—Elbert Hubbard

Overview

Once you have conducted a phone screen and concluded that the candidate is a potential fit for the role, it is time for the face-to-face interview. There are four parts to this step.

1. The welcome
2. The job overview investigation
3. The competency investigation
4. Setting expectations

Before we break down these four parts, let's take a moment to focus on our objective. In the MATCH process, the objective of the first interview is to determine if the candidate matches the job overview and the competency profile. The only way to achieve this objective is by collecting lots and lots of relevant information about

Sticky Notes:

- In an interview the candidate should do 90 percent of the talking.

- Script your interview questions using the job overview and the competency profile.

- Keep your ego out of it. Ask questions consistently from candidate to candidate.

the candidate, which you can do only by letting the candidate talk—a lot.

Too often, managers rush the process, trying too hard to sell the position, the company, and themselves at the risk of not really understanding the candidate. *Don't do that.* Your talking to listening ratio should be—ready for this?—90/10. (That is, the *candidate* should be talking 90 percent of the time). Ask your questions and then focus on listening, taking notes, and really *understanding* their answers.

Early in my recruiting career I worked with a hiring manager who chronically complained about his success rate. He told me many times that there just weren't enough qualified candidates. I knew what the problem was, but I was too much of a rookie to tell him that he talked too much.

Candidates would walk into his office for an interview. He would go on and on about where he went to school, where he started his career, and how he'd worked his way to the top. Then he'd describe—in painstaking detail—exactly what he wanted his new hire to do, and how he wanted it done. He'd spend 90 percent of the interview talking. Occasionally, he'd ask if there were any questions, only to quickly redirect the interview to a point of his choosing.

When it came to making an offer, desperate people would accept. Quality candidates were never interested. Somehow we managed to recruit a few performers in spite of his approach to hiring. If I recruited for him today, I would be compelled to tell him that he was standing in the way of solid hiring practices, though I doubt he would stop talking long enough to hear me.

The Interview Format and Your Hiring Team

People often ask me about the interviewing format:

- Which is better—a team or one-on-one interview?
- How long should an interview be?
- How many times should a candidate be interviewed?

- Which members of our team should be assigned to different aspects of the interview?
- How much time should be spent on the skills versus the competency fit questions?
- Should we give them a "skills test"?
- Should we have several people ask the candidate essentially the same questions and then compare the answers?

The answer to all of these questions is the same: let your hiring team customize the answer based on the role you are trying to fill. The only steadfast rule is to set the criteria and then stay *consistent*. Keeping the process constant throughout the hiring process is critical. You must emerge from your series of interviews with as much objective data as possible.

The Proper Attitude

Interviewers need to guard against the tendency to allow their preoccupation with the day's work to interfere with their candidate interaction. Fifteen minutes before the interview, pull out the candidate's résumé—along with your scripted job overview and competency fit questions—and review them. Prepare yourself to focus solely on the potential employee you are about to meet.

Your attitude during the interview should be friendly, inquisitive, and nonjudgmental. You're there to gather and understand information and present your company in the best light. Though your demeanor should be generally encouraging, you also need to be firm. Direct the course of the conversation to ensure that it stays focused and covers your priorities in the allotted time. In addition, in order to truly understand the candidate's responses, you may need to press for details. This can get uncomfortable, so be ready for it.

Five Tips for a Successful Interview

The following tips will help the interview process go smoothly.

Tip 1: Script Your Questions

If you've done any interviewing at all, you know that feeling of suddenly realizing you're almost out of time and you haven't gotten through a quarter of the areas you had planned on covering. You may have had a delightful conversation, but you don't have the information needed to determine the candidate's fit. Scripting helps keep you on track and prevents you from getting too distracted by a candidate's charisma.

Some hiring managers avoid scripting their interview questions. They figure they'll just go with the flow and ask whatever questions come to them. You can take that approach, of course. But chances are that if you make hiring decisions based on feeding your hunches with spontaneous conversation—with little genuine information to support your decision—you will get spotty results. I know; I see it all the time. What's *especially* dangerous about this approach is that it gets your ego wrapped up in the hire. The person you choose ends up becoming more than a hire; they become the evidence of your ability to judge people. If they *don't* work out, it reflects poorly on you. I've seen managers hang on to employees far longer than they should, costing the company both morale and money, because they were essentially too embarrassed to own up to their bad decision.

Remember, the MATCH process is about **excellence** in hiring. If you want to hire at the 100 percent success rate, then you must do the things that are required at that level of excellence. That means subsuming your ego to the process of objectively gathering information. Scripting is a great aid to keep your focus on the *process*.

Print out your questions, and leave lots of room for notes. I recommend attaching them to a clipboard, so that you can sit with the clipboard angled on the edge of the table or desk and take notes without the candidate reading them.

Tip 2: Use the Candidate's Name

As Dale Carnegie said, "Remember that a man's name is to him the sweetest and most important sound in the English language."

Use the candidate's name regularly (but naturally) in order to build rapport. You can do this with the tone of your voice by emphasizing the point of your question while including their name almost casually. Say this sentence aloud as a test while stressing the part in bold: "So, Melissa, what would you say has been your **greatest accounting challenge** over the past two years?" Can you hear how unforced Melissa's name flows within the question? You're using her name without drawing attention to the fact that you're doing so as a conscious interviewing technique.

Tip 3: Maintain Eye Contact

Maintaining eye contact during the interviewing process can be challenging since you also take notes.

Let's first talk about eye contact. Networking experts tell us that one good way to maintain natural eye contact is to focus on just *one* of the other person's eyes. It doesn't matter which; just pick one and stick with it. Unless you're sitting just an inch or two from the other person, they can't really tell you're looking at just one eye. If you're uncomfortable with eye contact, focus your thoughts on finding out and noting the color of the other person's eyes. That thought will make the exercise more analytical and less intimidating.

You want to be careful, of course, to avoid turning attentive eye contact into a psychotic staring contest. You can do this in a number of ways: looking at the person's *other* eye for a little while, nodding, blinking, and leaning forward or backward all help keep the eye contact looking natural. Also, it's perfectly acceptable for you to glance away for a few seconds when *you're* talking.

Maintaining eye contact is especially important at the points during the interview where you're covering crucial areas. Keeping eye contact when you ask, "So where did you go to college?" is not nearly as important as doing so when you ask, "When was the last time your integrity was challenged? What did you do in that situation?"

Tip 4: Take Notes

Good, detailed notes are critical to evaluating candidates. Your notes should contain factual information (e.g., has/does not have the skill) as well as your impressions (e.g., good storyteller/didn't take cue to wrap it up). Don't leave recollection to your memory. For the sake of the hiring team—and your own sanity—write it *all* down.

Taking notes is a real challenge when you're trying to also listen carefully and maintain eye contact. If needed, you may have an admin or another team member take notes. You may also record the interview (with permission from the candidate, of course); however, keep in mind that recording tends to formalize the atmosphere and can stifle honest, open interaction.

The key to taking good notes is to leave a 15-minute time slot open at the end of the interview session for you to reflect privately on the session and record your observations and impressions. If you allot this time in your planning, then you can write short, keyword notes during the interview that will trigger your full thoughts afterward. For example, you may ask your candidate about his project management experience, and he may tell you a story about managing a team through a SAP module implementation where he was responsible for five people and delivered the project a month behind schedule. You may jot down: *"story—SAP imp.—managed 5 ppl—delayed/gathering requirements from Cleveland office—GOOD— noted what he could have done differently (involved sr. mgmt sooner)—has req. experience."* Using these notes, you should be able to reconstruct the conversation and write it in a way that's clear to the rest of the hiring team.

Make sure to list only three or four questions per page. This format should leave you lots of white space in which to write. Remember, you want to build rapport and maintain as much eye contact as possible, so try to take notes without focusing on the page (ideally, without looking at it, depending on your penmanship).

Try to take notes fairly constantly throughout the interview or at least at regular intervals. You want to avoid having the candidate think that any one thing he or she has said is particularly critical. If you're writing frequently, you won't tip your hand.

Tip 5: Use Cues

Encourage the candidate to elaborate on answers and issues by using verbal and nonverbal cues. Using cues is important for a couple of reasons. First, it allows you to more easily manage the 90/10 candidate-to-interviewer talking ratio. Second, how a candidate reacts (or doesn't react) to a cue can tell you a lot about their interpersonal skills.

Below is a list of effective nonverbal and verbal tools. Although the list is rather obvious, the point here is that you want to consciously integrate these cues into the interviewing process:

Verbal Cues	Nonverbal Cues
"Uh-huh"	Nod head
"Hmmm"	Silence
"Go on"	Lean forward
"And then?"	Lean back in chair

The Four Parts of the Interview Process

There are four parts to the interview process. The process and the players can vary at the discretion of the hiring team, but for simplicity the sections are written from the perspective of one interviewer involved in a single, all-encompassing interview.

Part One: The Welcome

Before the first "hello," take a moment to compose yourself. Check the candidate's folder to make sure you have the résumé and the script. Take a deep breath, and focus your thoughts on the interview. Prepare yourself to listen like a hockey goalie waiting on the puck. Become an observer, noting the communications style of the candidate—from their handshake to their eye contact. Your job is to be a blank slate, never leading the witness, but instead allowing the potential employee to be him- or herself.

Set a warm tone by welcoming the candidate and engaging in two to three minutes of small talk. Your job is to create an environment in which the candidate feels comfortable opening up to you. You also want to discern if they are capable of informal, personal conversation; beware the person who either can't stop the chitchat or who insists on immediately "getting down to brass tacks."

Here are a few examples of good small-talk starters to use as you are settling into the interview:

- Were you able to find us without any problem?
- I haven't been outside today—how is the weather?
- I see from your résumé that you went to [name of college]; how did you like living in [name of college town]?

After a few minutes of small talk, it is time to transition into the core of the interview. I have provided a sample script which I have found to be effective in moving from the welcome to the skills investigation.

Well, let's get started. Today I am going to ask you a series of question about your skills, as well as your cultural preference in a company. As we discussed, this process will take approximately two hours. We will focus on both your strengths and your weaknesses. We believe that just as there is no perfect company, there is no perfect person. The best we can do is to align strengths with strengths. By doing this, we believe that we enable our employees to more effectively reach their career goals. Does this sound logical?

My questions will focus almost exclusively on your past accomplishments. In some cases, I will ask you to delve deeply into your past experiences. If you are unsure about the level of detail needed, don't hesitate to simply ask if I need more information. I recognize that you are a busy person, so if you are going into too much detail, I'll let you know so that we can conclude this process in the two-hour span.

Again, we have found this systematic way of evaluating people to be very effective. By sticking with this process we ensure that our new hires will be successful and happy. Do you have any further questions? Okay, let's get started.

Part Two: The Job Overview Investigation

The job overview investigation should be factual and objective. You should be able to ask about experience and skills, and then, after the response, discern with certainty whether the candidate possesses the ability to effectively carry out the duties of the job. Unlike the competency investigation that follows this step, the job overview investigation rarely requires you to make a judgment call.

Preparation for the Job Overview Investigation

Since the most obviously unqualified candidates should have been weeded out during the phone screen, you'll explore a deeper level of detail in the job overview investigation.

You will already have the job description and the required skills as laid out in the job overview. The hiring team will have set requirements for the position along with the relative "weighting" of each skill, so you know which skills are critical and which ones are nice-to-haves. The next step in preparation, then, is to more clearly define your terms—not only for yourself, but for others on your interview team.

Take a skill set requirement such as "the candidate must have working knowledge of spreadsheet applications." Consider: how exactly do you define "working knowledge"? Is it knowing how to:

- Enter data and format?
- Enter formulas? If so, which kinds?
- Run pivot tables? You may consider pivot tables part of "working knowledge," while others may consider them an advanced skill.

The same approach applies to harder to clarify skills, such as "must be able to manage a small team." The word *manage* is broad;

it can encompass everything from visioning to counseling to budg-
eting. Be clear on what, in your opinion, constitutes being "able
to manage," as well as what number of people you consider to be
"small" (three to four? nine to ten?).

The exercise of precisely defining your terms should serve to
feed the next, deeper level of questions. For example, once the
team agrees that "being able to manage" means being able to plan
a multi-month implementation using Microsoft Project, managing
the tasks and resources, presenting the milestones, and interfacing
with at least one other business unit, then the actual questions you
ask the candidate should fall naturally out of that definition.

Another source for developing detailed skills questions will be
your phone screen notes. The responses to those questions naturally lend themselves to a detailed follow-up.

Measurement

Developing the *measurement* of each of the skills is closely aligned
with defining your terms. You need to know if indeed the candidate possesses a given skill. And just as some skills are easier to
define than others, some are easier to measure than others. You
can sit down with a candidate and ask him or her to go through
a spreadsheet test and see right away whether they know their stuff.
However, when it comes to skills like managing, your approach will
involve a series of open-ended questions to understand exactly what
the candidate has done. In addition, your references check will help
to round out your assessment. Remember, however, that your measurements for the skills should drive you to a clear yes or no.

Interviewing Skills

While silences can be awkward, so can situations where you have to
press the candidate for more information. You don't want to come
across as a police interrogator, but you may find yourself repeating
the same question more than once, or asking clarifying questions
because the candidate has not answered them to your satisfaction.

Without clear definitions and measurements, your interview can easily unravel. Even *with* them, you run the risk of not getting enough information to make a sound decision. If you do need more information, ask for it straightaway. The candidate's reaction can tell you a lot, especially about their communication skills.

Getting a candidate to open up and give you enough information can be challenging, but so can the other extreme.

Talking Too Much

What do you do when you ask, in effect, what time it is, and the candidate tells you how to build a watch?

Occasionally, even with all your interview tools—verbal and nonverbal cues, a very clear introduction, and a well-written script—you will interview a candidate who talks too much. I have met my fair share of these candidates. Some of them are just naturally garrulous, some are nervous, some believe they're really helping you out by disclosing a large amount of detail, and some are just not good at picking up on cues to wrap it up. Keep in mind that how much a person talks has *very little* to do with their ability to do the job. In fact, this area is one where interviewers who don't follow a hiring process make mistakes. They pass on perfectly good candidates because their communication styles are mismatched.

Here is how I suggest you handle the loquacious interviewee. First, provide a simple reminder: *I appreciate the level of detail you are giving me, but please work on summarizing your points.*

If the long-winded answers continue, remind the candidate of the ground rules you set:

[Candidate], please remember that when we started this interview process, I stated that our goal was to complete the interview in two hours. The length of your answers won't allow us to cover all the critical areas we need to work through, so please limit your answers to two minutes.

If the individual continues with the same long-windedness, I suggest one more polite reminder. The candidate should apologize and try to correct themselves. If they don't, then jot that in your notes as a point to discuss with your hiring team.

Qualifying: Why a Job Change at This Time?

A good way to transition from the skills section of the interview to the next section—the competency fit investigation—is to explore the question, "Why are you exploring a job change at this time?" Understanding the reason behind a job change is so critical that there is no reason to move forward with the interview process until you do.

Some people make a move for reasons completely unrelated to job satisfaction; they've just moved to the city, their current company is going out of business or downsizing, and so forth. In those cases, the reference check will play a large role in understanding the candidate.

However, the candidate may express some dissatisfaction with his or her current state, either personally, professionally, or a combination of both. Most candidates will lead the interview with their professional reasons for leaving and will generally have a rehearsed answer like, "I'm looking for opportunities to grow." This response is worth exploring with follow-up questions. Listen specifically for:

- Areas of disagreement between the candidate and his or her immediate supervisor. Are the areas personal? Philosophical?
- Their line of reasoning—is their rationale sound?
- How the candidate talks about his or her company. Does the candidate "respectfully disagree"?
- The amount of initiative the candidate showed in resolving the issues.
- The amount of emphasis on adding value versus the amount of finding out "what's in it for me." The answer's undercurrent should be something like, "I know I am capable of more. I know I can add more value."

That last bullet point cannot be stressed enough. You want people who are focused on contributing to your company's success— people who rise above any petty politics and find the resources and initiatives to get things done.

There are two categories of reasons for changing jobs: Red Flags and Valid Career Wounds. Here are some examples of both:

Red flags	Valid Career Wounds
More money	Not enough responsibility
Blaming a boss	Change in culture due to acquisition, change in management, etc.
Entitlement	Inability to use a new degree or certification
Expected recognition for merely performing one's job	Lack of recognition for exceptional work
Complaints about nonexcessive overtime	Excessive overtime

Writing from Atlanta, I would add another valid career wound: commute time. A drive that took less than an hour five years ago can take three or more hours these days. While cell phoning and audio books are wonderful diversions from the commuter blues, spending three hours a day in a car is simply too much to ask.

Dig Deep

A job change is a life-altering event and not something that anyone should take lightly. Probe the reasoning behind "why now" so that you can gain real insight into what motivates the candidate. Remember, the candidate is trying to put on their best face on the interview; keep digging. Let's review this typical exchange:

Interviewer: So, Bill, you said you aren't satisfied with your current situation. Can you tell me a little more about that?

Bill: Sure. Well, I just got my MBA and I want to apply it.

Interviewer: And why aren't you able to utilize your new skills in your current role?

Bill: As an assistant controller, I just don't have the opportunity to manage people.

Interviewer: Have you talked to the controller about this?

Bill: Absolutely, but she isn't going anywhere. She told me that she has been with the company for 12 years, and expects to be the controller for 12 more.

Interviewer: Are there other places where you could grow in your ability to manage?

Bill: Not within this department. I might be able to transfer to Tennessee, but that won't work for our family at this time.

Interviewer: So, what you are saying is that you want to apply the management skills that you learned while working on your MBA, but in your current role you are unable to do so, *and* there is no opportunity for management in a reasonable period of time? Is there anything I missed?

Bill: No.

Interviewer: Is there anything else that would compel you to change jobs at this time?

Bill: No. Other than that I love my job and the people I work with. It will be tough to leave them, but I think it is the right thing to do for my career and personal growth plan.

The saying goes that an employee does not quit a company: he or she quits a boss or a department. What you're getting at with the question, "Why are you changing jobs at this time?" is an understanding of this person's values and personality. This will help you better decide if the candidate is a fit for your position.

Part Three: The Competency Investigation

Whereas skills can be answered with a clear "yes" or "no," the competency investigation delves into gray areas: *What is the candidate's management style? How collaborative is he or she? What is their degree of comfort with confrontation?* Evaluating the answers to these questions requires some judgment on your part, as well as careful discussion by and consensus from your hiring team.

Back in step three (creating the competency profile), you worked through the personal competencies of your ideal employee.

You prioritized these values, and developed your list of behavioral questions for the candidate. This list will keep the interview focused and moving forward. However, I would caution you on three points:

- **Be aware of time.** Open-ended behavioral questions like the ones you'll ask are often answered with stories. Stories are great, provided they give you the insight you need to assess the specific competency. However, stories can also veer off on a tangent that, while valuable to the candidate, may do little to advance the interview. It's important—but not always easy—to distinguish between useful information and fluff. As you listen to a response, keep in mind what you're trying to measure. Use follow-up questions and nonverbal cues to remain on point.

- **Be specific enough with your questions without revealing your intent.** Don't lead the witness. Rather than saying, *"I'm interested in how effective your communication skills are,"* you can say, *"Tell me about some of the feedback you've received on your communication style."* Use the candidate response to drill down to your main concern.

- **Avoid hypotheticals.** Consider an opening like, *"Tell me about your decision-making process."* The candidate should be able to outline the general process he or she uses, and then cite an example or two from their own experience. Remember, this section of the interview should focus on *actual* past behavior, responsibility, and results. You want to avoid asking hypothetical questions, and be equally wary when you receive an answer couched in hypothetical terms: *"Well, if I **were** making a big decision, I would . . ."* No. You're not interested in what they *would* do. *Anything* is possible hypothetically. You're interested in hearing examples of what they *did* do.

To realize the most benefit from your limited time with the candidate, ensure that the entire team takes careful and copious notes. When the series of interviews has concluded, the team will reconvene to discuss the candidate's personality fit. Having well-documented, structured data will allow the team to share objective data and make the best decision possible.

Part Four: Setting Expectations

Once the interview is over, it is your job to set expectations for what is to follow. A good interviewer will remain upbeat and positive without making any promises. In most cases, it is a good idea to ask the candidate to follow up at a prescribed time in order to test his or her interest in the position.

My suggested script in setting expectations is as follows:

. . . *that concludes our interview. I want to thank you so much for your thoughtful responses.*

Our next steps are for me to go to the hiring team and to report on your answers. Depending on their conclusions, we will ask you back for a second interview, which will include an office visit as well as some time with you and HR to go over our benefits program.

To find out if you'll be asked back for a second interview, please call _____ on Wednesday of next week at 4:00 PM. Thanks again for your interest in _____.

A Final Word: Where to Interview?

Let me leave you with a tip as we transition to the next chapter: instead of meeting in the same place for every interview, mix it up. Meet in your office for the first interview, the conference room next, and a coffee shop for the third meeting. For management positions, I strongly advise dinner meetings with spouses. Sports events, concerts, and the golf course are other ideal places to get to know your candidates.

11

Check References

Step 7

The ability to make good decisions regarding people represents one of the last reliable sources of competitive advantage since very few organizations are very good at it.

—Peter Drucker

O nce the candidate's interview is completed, you're now ready to check his or her references. The purpose of this step is to independently validate the information that you've collected during the interviews. You'll also have the opportunity to explore new areas of the candidate's skills and personality. The reference check should serve as a continuation of the MATCH process—confirming or denying key points that have been identified in the recruiting effort.

Demand multiple references from your candidates. You need to contact references who have worked on the same level as the candidate, peers, and those who supervised the candidate. For a critical hire, contact references at all levels going back 10 years. While this might seem a bit like overkill, you'll gather significant data as you strive to hire and then effectively manage the new employee.

Prior to the Reference Call

Work with the candidate to determine the best way to approach a reference. It is considered proper etiquette for the candidate to provide contact information and a best time to call. If a reference is uncomfortable about discussing the candidate while they're at work, arrange to call them at home. Assure references that their comments will remain confidential. (This book does not focus on the legal aspects of checking a reference, so be sure to confirm guidelines with your human resources [HR] team.)

A reference call should never be a surprise. The candidate should contact each of his or her references so that your call will be expected, and hopefully welcomed. Failure to introduce your call should be noted and considered by the hiring team.

Reference calls are too often—and incorrectly—handled as a clerical function. Whenever possible, the hiring manager, or at least someone who has been trained in behavioral techniques, should conduct the reference checks. This is, after all, a key element in the process of truly understanding the candidate you are considering.

Start Broad and End Narrow

Think of your reference call as an inverted triangle—one that starts with generalities and moves toward details. Reference calls too frequently focus on specific skills, with little to no attention paid to the candidate's personality and cultural proclivity. An effective reference process starts with a very broad view before focusing on specifics.

Cover Skills and Competencies

Through the MATCH process you created a job overview and isolated core competencies. You've systematically incorporated these key areas into your candidate interview; now, let the same priorities guide your reference calls. Skills that required thorough investigation in the interview process also require thorough investigation during the reference check. This is equally true with the competency profile. If "integrity" was a key competency in the interview process, then it deserves equal billing during the reference check.

Behavioral Questioning in the Reference Check

You should utilize behavioral-oriented questioning for references just as you did for interviewing. Asking a reference to "rank the candidate's managerial skills from 1 to 10, with 10 being the highest," is still a worthless reality for all too many reference calls. Compare this line of inquiry to the far more illuminating: "Describe the candidate's management style." There is really no comparison, especially when mixed in with great follow-up questions such as, "Describe the last time the candidate lost his/her temper with an employee," or "How did the staff respond when the candidate was out of the office for an extended period?"

A Suggested Reference Call Script

Hello, _____, my name is _____ and I am calling from _____. I know that _____ reached out to you in regards to my reference call, and he/she suggested that this would be a good time for you. Is that correct—do you have roughly 30 minutes to discuss _____?

We are considering _____ for the role of _____ with our organization. But in order to go any further, we need to better understand his/her work style and skills. Our philosophy is that, just as there is no perfect company, there is no perfect employee; our job is to work to align the strengths of the individual with the strengths of the organization; therefore, we'll need to focus not only on what the candidate does best, but also areas that need improvement. What I'd like to do today is to start very broad—trying to get a better idea of how you see _____, and then move into specifics. Is that okay with you? Great, let's get started then.

First, let me understand exactly your relationship with _____. Can you please clarify when and where you worked with _____ and in what capacity you worked together? Great. Thanks for clarifying that.

Now, what is one word you would use to describe _____? Why did you choose that word?

Please describe _____'s working style.

What is _____ *'s greatest strength?*

What is _____ *'s greatest weakness?*

(Note: In my experience, most people do not like to talk about a candidate's weakness. A typical response is "[the candidate] didn't have any weaknesses." My suggestion is to remain quiet after this response. The silence almost always elicits a truthful response.)

Where do you see _____ *in two years? In five years?*

What is the highest point you see _____ *reaching in his/her career? Why do you say that?*

Now, let's get a little more specific. I am now going to ask some questions that focus on _____ *'s personality. We've identified some key competencies that have led to the following questions:*

This phase of the reference call requires you to rely on the work the hiring team did in identifying and prioritizing. In most circumstances, you should try to stick to 30 minutes per call. To maximize the reference's time, attempt to limit your behavioral questions to only key areas. To exemplify, let's assume that the hiring team has decided that the top five competencies are: (1) capable of translating corporate goals to reality, (2) integrity, (3) delegation, (4) ability to hire and fire, and (5) stress management. Following are suggested behavioral questions for each category:

1. Capable of translating corporate goals to reality:
   - Tell me about _____'s track record of translating corporate goals to reality.
   - When was the last instance in which _____ missed a goal that was critical to the organization?
2. Integrity:
   - When was the last time that _____'s integrity was challenged?
   - How did he/she react?
   - What was the outcome?
3. Delegation:
   - Give me a story where _____ utilized his/her team in completing a project?
   - When has _____ had to take over work from a person that is lower on the organizational chart?

4. The ability to hire and fire:
    - When did you observe _____ hire an employee? What were the results of the hire?
    - What was _____'s best hire? What was _____'s worst hire?
    - When did you observe _____ fire an employee? What were the steps that led to the firing?
    - By firing the employee was the organization strengthened or weakened?

5. Stress management:
    - What does _____ do to effectively manage stress?
    - When was the last time you saw _____ ineffectively manage stress?

The third portion of the reference call should be focused on skills. This will give you the opportunity to ask very specific questions. Again, strive to make these questions behavioral in nature, not simple "yes/no" questions. For instance, instead of asking: *"On a scale of 1 to 10, how would you describe _____'s ability to use Oracle?"* ask: *"In what capacity did _____ use Oracle? What was his/her greatest accomplishment in using Oracle to achieve business objectives?"*

Once you have satisfied your prioritized objectives in this portion of the reference, move toward closing out the call. I suggest the following script:

"We are currently considering _____ for the position of _____. In this role she/he will be responsible for _____, _____, and _____. She/he will be managing a total of _____. The positions she/he will be responsible for will be _____, _____, and _____. He/she will report to _____. What are your thoughts on this candidate for this role?"

And, finally, never forget the final reference question. In my years as an executive recruiter, I have learned more about candidates with this simple question than any other.

"Thanks for your time today. Is there anything else that I have missed that I should know about this candidate?"

As you are conducting your references, it is imperative that you take copious notes. Asking these questions without doing so will be of little value to your hiring team. Relying on your memory is completely counter to the MATCH process.

How to Get a Reference to Return Your Call Every Time

When I was new to the world of executive recruiting, I had a hard time getting people to call me back on references. Now I get a return call rate of nearly 100 percent. There are two keys to ensuring that you'll get a call back:

1. **Delegate responsibility.** Inform the candidate that it is common courtesy to proactively prepare a reference for your call. This way, you know you won't be calling out of the blue. (By the way, this step provides an additional opportunity for you to determine your candidate's interest level. If you ask the candidate to call and later find out that he or she did not, then this is something you should seriously consider.)
2. **Leave an effective voice mail.** *"Please call me so that I can conduct a reference on _____"* sounds about as appealing as your dentist reminding you to come in for a filling. Try something like this: *"Hi, this is Dan Erling with _____. I had the opportunity to talk with _____ about an opportunity with our organization. She/he is being highly considered, but I'll need to talk with you before we can move forward. I believe that she/he has reached out to explain the nature and urgency of my call. I am looking forward to discussing _____ at your earliest possible convenience. I will be in the office this afternoon, and I will prioritize your call."*

Using the Data Collected in the Reference Calls

As we have discussed throughout the book, the MATCH process allows us to objectively isolate and compare behaviors, allowing you to make a logical hiring decision. If the reference process has been conducted correctly, the data will be imperative in determining the best candidate available for the job. References can be used to:

- Confirm or refute strengths and weaknesses that you uncover during the candidate interview process.
- Unearth strengths and weaknesses that were *not* uncovered in the interview process.
- Collect objective observations of the candidate's cultural proclivity, work style, personality, and skills to be used when considering the best fit for the role.
- Determine the candidate's strength of network—something that is especially important for executive positions and relationship-based sales roles.
- Collect information that will be useful in managing/coaching the candidate.
- Collect information that will be useful for those whom the candidate will manage/coach.

The Value of References during the Interview Process

Sometimes the "threat" of a reference check will elicit great information from a candidate, which can be even more valuable than that obtained from the actual reference. During the interview process, let the potential employee know that you will personally be conducting the references. If you have done a thorough job interviewing the candidate, then he or she will be expecting a reference check that is just as comprehensive. With this expectation in place, you are ready to ask a series of exceptionally revealing question:

- *"When I am conducting your reference, I will focus both on your strengths and weaknesses. What do you expect your references to tell me?"*
- *"When I inquire about areas where you need to improve, how do you think they will respond?"*

And while this is not a reference question, I suggest you close this section of the interview with:

- "On top of references, almost 100 percent of companies do a thorough background check. Is there anything we *should* proactively discuss in preparation for a barrage of checks?"

By inquiring in this fashion, you will be able to learn a great deal about your potential employee.

Perform Background Checks

Step 8

Trust, but verify.

—Ronald Reagan

W hen I began recruiting in the late 1990s, our clients very infrequently requested background checks. In fact, I can remember doing only about 12 per *year*. These days, we are asked to run dozens of background checks each *week*. It is considered the norm to use a background check to evaluate a criminal history, credit record, driving record, and drug use.

Due to the sensitivity of information, there are a variety of laws governing background checks. Most notably, the Fair Credit Reporting Act protects people from the misuse of these easy-to-access records. Employers must show equality in administering background checks; for instance, if you require one candidate to complete a credit check, then you have to ask all candidates to do the same.

I have found that 50 percent of résumés contain some distortion of the truth. It is therefore important that you make background

Sticky Notes:

- Background checks are inexpensive and easy to administer.

- Focus background checks on areas pertinent to your hire.

- When conducting an education check, be sure you have the candidate's name while they were attending college.

checks part of the MATCH process. Here is a partial list of background checks that are available to you:

- Criminal, arrest, incarceration, and sex offender records
- Citizenship, immigration, or legal working status
- Litigation records
- Driving and vehicle records
- Drug tests
- Education records
- Employment records
- Financial information

Please note that this is not intended to be a legal handbook. In conducting any sort of background checks, make sure you are working with a well-established, reputable firm that can assist you on all the legal ramifications of making decisions based on a candidate's background.

MATCH

The Process:
Phase III

Executing the Hire

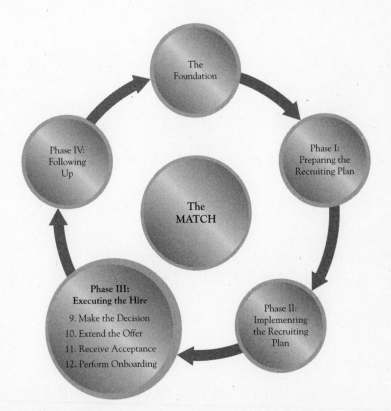

If the recruiting plan was implemented thoroughly and consistently, you'll enjoy the benefits during this next phase. Executing the hire takes you through the last mile of the hiring process, from making the candidate decision through extending the offer. The process does not stop at the hiring decision point; indeed, the MATCH process covers acceptance and onboarding, as these steps are vital to setting the candidate on a path to long-term success.

13

Make the Decision

Step 9

You will either step forward into growth or you will step back into safety.
—Abraham Maslow

I t's decision time. Without a systemic process a hiring manager can feel as if they are about to launch wildly into the vast unknown, flailing blindfolded and alone. By contrast, following the steps of the MATCH process allows the hiring manager to feel as if they are about to make a short leap with eyes wide open, with the hiring team at their side.

The intention of this book is to make your leap of faith as small as possible. Each step of the MATCH process has raised your odds of hiring the right person. The tools and processes in this book have allowed you to:

- Cover all aspects of hiring.
- Compare candidates uniformly.

If you've been following the steps in this book—developing the list of necessary skills and competencies, as well as being consistent in your questioning—you will have a very short list of qualified and interested candidates. Even if the actual decision occurs at some subconscious level, the steps you've just

Sticky Notes:

- If done correctly, the MATCH process will produce a pool of qualified and interested candidates.

- The candidate's immediate supervisor should be charged with the ultimate decision.

- Be as objective as possible, but accept that all decisions have an emotional component.

been through have given your inner processor clear and consistent information, along with unambiguous measures to evaluate that information.

You should feel confident about your choice. If team members disagree, the case for a particular candidate can be articulated through the job overview, the competency profile, and all the notes associated with the candidate pool. With this approach, you have a common structure with which to evaluate the candidates.

Responsibilities

Each member of the hiring team should provide input, but the vital roles in the decision-making process belong to:

- **The CEO.** Ultimate responsibility for hiring exceptional talent lies with the acting CEO. However, great CEOs rarely step in to veto a hire, nor do they use their power to sway a particular candidate. By instituting a step-by-step objective process, the CEO can rest assured that the hiring team is acting in the best interest of the organization. For hires at the executive level the CEO will be acting as the lead decision maker.
- **Human resources.** HR works best as the facilitator of the hiring process, not the final decision maker (unless, of course, the position is in the HR department). HR should help train the hiring team in the steps leading to this point. They should also moderate the final decision-making session. In our experience, HR shines when it guides others to help make the best decisions, but HR hampers efforts to build a unified team when they become final decision maker.
- **The candidate's immediate supervisor.** With counsel from HR, the CEO, and the affected department, the immediate supervisor should be the one to make the final hiring decision. For example, if the company is hiring an accounts payable clerk, the final hiring decision should be made by the accounts payable manager.

The Process

Gather together the original hiring team, the original job description, and the competencies. Bring notes from the interview process, reference checks, and the background checks.

The intent of the process is to revisit the whole landscape of hard skills, soft skills, and company culture, comparing the candidates' qualities as evenly as is possible. No candidate is a 100 percent fit, so you'll need to explore what their shortcomings mean for your company—more training? Shifted responsibilities?

In my experience, all other areas being satisfactory, the competency "fit" should hold sway. As I have noted before, people can be trained to develop skills. They can't be trained to fit the culture.

The candidate's immediate supervisor is at the center of the process. He or she needs to hear collected data from all sides: department members, the broader hiring team, and then the CEO or designee. If disagreements arise, HR should step in and ask questions that draw out the reasoning from all sides. Be especially sensitive to draw out the opinions of the quieter "type B's" in your group, as they often have insights into character issues that the less sensitive but more vocal type A's don't perceive.

Try to develop a meeting culture where no concerns are left unheard. Let it be known that no one will be held accountable for their opinion. Stress that each individual is responsible for discussing every angle of their concerns, even if they must play devil's advocate. Once everything is on the table, the candidate's immediate supervisor is charged with the responsibility of the hire. And although there may be those who disagree, it is the responsibility of the team to fully support the final decision.

If you follow the preceding process, the decision will often be obvious to all involved. The decision will still require that small leap of faith—gut decision, whatever you want to call it—but you'll make the decision having considered all of the criteria in a methodical process, which dramatically increases your chance for 100 percent success in your hiring efforts.

Extend the Offer

Step 10

There are two things people want more than sex and money—recognition and praise.

—Mary Kay Ash

A salary represents the perceived value of an employee's impact on a company. Negotiating that "value" can be tough. Discussions of money can be similar to discussions of politics in that they can bring out completely unpredictable personality dimensions.

The beauty of the MATCH process is that each progressive step has aligned the right people to the right job within your company. By this point your candidate pool should contain highly qualified candidates poised to accept your offer. Even so, to help with salary negotiations, ensure that base salary is only one aspect of any offer. There are two other dimensions to your offer:

Sticky Notes:

- A job offer should be presented as more than a base salary.

- Before making the offer, thoroughly research the candidate's salary history as well as market conditions.

- The MATCH process does not end when you extend the offer.

1. **The monetary value of the *total* package:** base salary + bonus + benefits + profit sharing + extras, like a company car. You should itemize and outline this total dollar amount for the candidate.
2. **The intangibles.** People are motivated by more than money, of course: growth potential, interesting work, and even the daily commute are factors that should be considered.

Knowing What to Offer

If a candidate has stated interest in a specific position, at a certain salary range, then it is safe to assume that the candidate will accept an offer within the range identified. However, human nature always seems to push expectations toward the upper end of a salary range. Rarely do we see candidates who don't expect their salary to be at the top of the range. Even the underqualified candidate applying for a position will assume that a salary range of $85,000 to $90,000 means they will be offered $90,000.

There are two simple ways to counter this tendency. First, from the onset of interviewing, limit conversations to career growth and competency fit—downplaying salary. This allows the candidate to recognize the truly important aspects of accepting a job, resulting in a candidate motivated by career growth instead of dollar signs. Second, either don't post a salary at all (though this may lead to other misunderstandings) or don't advertise the maximum salary range.

Occasionally, there will be a candidate who expects you to "fall in love" with their skills, lose rationality, and make an emotional hire. They have a salary history above the stated range, and expect your organization to recognize their uberqualifications and pay accordingly. Occasionally, the hiring team may decide on this course of action, but more often than not, it is better to stick to the budget (especially if the proper front-end due diligence has been conducted).

Salary history is crucial in knowing what to offer. Ideally, you are looking for a candidate who has had steady career progression leading to a current compensation slightly below your offered salary. As part of your background check, get salary history going back at least three jobs.

Market forces dictate the appropriate salary increase. As an executive recruiter I have seen times where a 30 percent increase was considered the norm in order to motivate a job transition. However, I have also been witness to times where a lateral move from a failing company to a growing company was the norm. This is a case where being in touch with the hiring market is invaluable. A solid relationship with a recruiter can provide an excellent source for current hiring trends.

As early as possible in the interview process, investigate the candidate's career goals. Money rarely is the exclusive factor in changing jobs—in fact, we believe that with great candidates money should be at least third (career growth and corporate culture should top the list). Use questioning techniques to identify the key to the hire—that thing that the candidate most desires in his or her next job (management responsibility, upward growth, title, location, etc.)

In cases where the candidate is being relocated, make sure to take into account different costs of living for different cities. For example, a person making $100,000 in Manhattan might be completely satisfied with $70,000 in Atlanta. But a person making $100,000 in Atlanta would have to make more than $150,000 to live comfortably in Los Angeles. Communicating the relative nature of housing, transportation, health care, and so on allows candidates to compare the salary you are offering and make a logical decision.

Offer and Counteroffer

So you put your offer to the candidate. They may ask for time to consider it. A day or two should suffice (certainly no more than a week except for the most unique cases). In the meantime, even if you don't expect it, prepare for a counteroffer in the form of requests for higher salary, more vacation, more bonus potential, or title. If the candidate does indeed counter your offer, work first to understand the candidate's reasoning. Take the time to thoroughly examine the counter before making your decision.

Occasionally, there is an impasse. However, as you become more and more adept at the MATCH process, you will find that impasses occur infrequently. There are two reasons for this decrease:

1. People will not go through a lengthy process if they are merely "kicking tires." It is human nature to wonder if the grass is indeed greener on the other side of the fence. However, it is not human nature to traverse an exhausting process of exploration simply to explore an opportunity.

2. The recruiting plan addresses the "root cause" of a candidate's desire for a job. Motivations are uncovered early on in the interview process. By clearly understanding the driving force behind a candidate's motivation for change (management experience, technical exposure, challenge, etc.), those motivating factors

can and should be focused upon in the job offer. For instance, if it has been established that the candidate is attracted to the position due to increased management responsibility, then make that clear in the offer.

But even in cases where the candidate has gone through the many steps of our process, and the offer has been made in a way that focuses on the goals that will be attained through acceptance, there still can be an impasse. When an impasse occurs, the first step is to listen. What stone was not turned over during the recruiting plan? What is causing the hesitation? Are you hitting a fear-of-change issue? Does the candidate have a valid reason for stalling? If so, make the necessary adjustment so that the offer will be accepted. If you determine that the counter is not acceptable, never be afraid to walk from the deal. Except in the rarest of circumstances, there are other fish in the sea. Fear of losing a candidate is never a good point from which to negotiate.

Assuming you do agree on a salary, confirm everything in writing: a letter stating the start date, salary, vacation days, bonus plan, and anything else that was discussed and agreed to should be included in your offer letter. If there are legal aspects to your agreement, include them in your letter, but start off with a welcoming tone and then move to legalese.

One quick note on the value of high-quality recruiting firms: if you're really stuck on the fairness of an offer, call a recruiting firm. They work the market every day. At my firm, we keep a database of the actual salaries paid to our candidates, cross-referenced with position, level, industry, and company size. We are often asked to help negotiate offers because, as a third party, we can present the case objectively.

You're Still Only 90 Percent There

As you'll see in the next chapter, it ain't over till it's over, and that's especially true with the hiring process. Hiring can be like a thriller movie: you think you've been through the worst. You think it's over. You relax, and then . . . bang! There's still that one last twist they throw in, just for the thrill. In the case of hiring, of course, you're *in* the movie (in fact, you're one of the main characters), so you better be prepared for whatever comes your way.

CHAPTER 15

Receive Acceptance

Step 11

It is not the strongest of the species that survive, nor the most intelligent, but the one most responsive to change.

—Charles Darwin

C hange is difficult—for everyone. Psychologists rank "starting a new job" third, just below "death of a loved one" and "divorce" on the stress continuum. So even though you and the hiring team have agreed on a candidate, remember that the deal still faces major obstacles, and if you don't manage the emotional "care and feeding" of your candidate during the transition to your company, you could easily lose them.

A Glimpse into the Other Side

We'll talk about what you can do in a moment, but let me first give you insight into what happens at the candidate's current company, once they turn in their notice. (Or maybe you already know, because you do this in your own company!)

1. Upon telling their supervisor that they are resigning to go to work for your company, that supervisor says something like, "Let's keep this news between you and me until we can make a formal announcement."

Sticky Notes:

- Accept that changing jobs is extremely stressful for your candidate.

- Plan for the possibility of a counteroffer.

- Keep in frequent touch with small pieces of information.

2. The president or the CEO personally calls to invite the resigning employee out to dinner.
3. At dinner, the bigwig praises the resigning employee and mentions that he or she was being seriously considered for a raise and promotion. The bigwig explains that it is really a shame that he or she is leaving when such great plans were in the works.
4. The resigning employee is approached the next day and asked to reconsider their notice. A new compensation package is offered, and sometimes a new title and new responsibilities. During the talent war days (late 1990s) we even saw a brand new Harley-Davidson offered in a counteroffer package.

Given most candidate's natural aversion to change, the counteroffer can be very tempting.

For the record, many times the counter offering company is simply stalling. We have seen many candidates take the counteroffer and wind up out of a job in three months. After all, a lack of loyalty has been shown. That is not to say that all counteroffers are bad—we have seen deals that worked out well. When asked for advice on this matter, we ask the candidate to remember what it was that initiated the desire to leave in the first place. Money can temporarily make our situation feel better, but the underlying reasons that drove us to look at other opportunities usually reemerge after a short period of time.

What You Can Do

As discussed earlier in this book, one of the best ways to make sure you're hiring a solid candidate is to confirm that they're looking for career growth and a good work situation, not just more money. You don't want to get into a bidding war, nor do you want candidates who will make decisions with money as their top priority. If you're sure you offer the best work situation for the candidate, that puts you on good footing to close the deal. With that clarified, here is the suggested acceptance process:

- Have the CEO (or the highest ranking person on the hiring team) call with an enthusiastic congratulations.
- Follow that call with a call from the candidate's immediate supervisor, welcoming the candidate as a new hire.

- Send out the offer letter immediately. Send by email, and then follow up with a letter, preferably with a handwritten note.
- Set and agree upon a start date.
- Develop a communications plan for the interim that involves not only HR, but the candidate's new department. Remember, you must do everything you can to help ease the emotional stress of switching jobs.
  - ○ Have HR send a list of benefits, then set up a time to talk one on one about the benefits program.
  - ○ Have the supervisor send a policy manual. Again, set up a time to talk about it.
  - ○ Invite the candidate to a company event, and introduce him or her to people throughout the company.
  - ○ Send them a formal invitation to the company's holiday party.
  - ○ Assign a mentor (not the supervisor) to assist in the transition to the new company. Encourage the pair to have lunch together (company sponsored) before the start date.

Now that the candidate is on board, you could send all the paperwork in one big packet, but we've found it's better to use a drip approach as a way of welcoming the candidate and introducing them to a variety of people. Do whatever you can to begin looping your new hire into the culture of the department and the company. Marketers say that people make decisions initially with their emotions, and then they justify their emotional decisions with reason and facts. The more you reinforce the candidate's decision to leave, the more comfortable they'll feel about that decision.

In the recruiting business, we pay especially close attention to the period between acceptance and the first day the candidate actually shows up at their new company. Our recruiters talk to the candidate three or four times a week, discussing logistics and paperwork, but more importantly—constantly reassuring the candidate that (1) their decision is correct, and (2) change is difficult for everyone, so any apprehension they have is not a sign that they made the wrong decision—it's a normal part of the process. Your team should reinforce those messages, too.

16

Perform Onboarding

Step 12

The most valuable asset of a 21st century institution will be its knowledge workers and their productivity.

—Peter Drucker

Employees should be treated as you would treat volunteers. If you've ever been in charge of rounding up a group of people to do a project in their free time, you know what I mean. You treat your volunteers like gold. You express your gratitude when they join your team. You do everything you can to help them succeed. You check in on them as they're working. And you thank them sincerely when they're done.

Interesting how the interaction changes when a paycheck is inserted. You don't have volunteers. You have employees, and employees have job descriptions, and they have reviews. If they don't perform up to snuff, they can be terminated.

That mentality worked marginally well back in the assembly line era. Let's face it, as long as the quota of nuts got screwed onto bolts, it didn't really matter how the worker felt about his or her job.

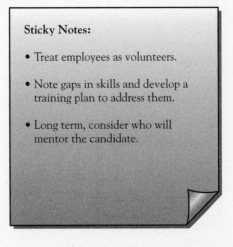

Sticky Notes:

• Treat employees as volunteers.

• Note gaps in skills and develop a training plan to address them.

• Long term, consider who will mentor the candidate.

However, today we live in an economy where ideas rule. Paychecks don't buy ideas. Paychecks buy bodies and a minimal set of tasks. The best parts of people—their creativity, their caring, their personal commitment to the success of your company—those are volunteered by happy and engaged workers.

Your new employee is about to arrive. Will they be treated like a worker expected to punch the clock, or a "volunteer"?

The Process

A strong onboarding program is the chance for the candidate to become acclimated to the company culture. If you have gone through your hiring process correctly, then there will be few surprises. The candidate's strengths and weaknesses will jibe with the strengths and weaknesses of the company. It also sets the table for retention (our next chapter).

Even the most solid onboarding process will not make up for a misaligned hire. I learned this lesson early in my recruiting career. A terrific company with excellent benefits, a wonderful company culture, and a well-established onboarding program hired an energetic, bright, well-educated tax accountant to run their tax department. This candidate had exactly the background they needed and was dead-on in their price range.

I couldn't figure out why, two months into the hire, the candidate was miserable and the company was sure that something was not right. The candidate quit and went back to his former company, where he was welcomed with open arms, going back to a very productive role.

Unfortunately, as a rookie recruiter I underestimated the power of the corporate fit and overestimated the power of a solid onboarding process. While the candidate had the perfect skills, the culture was not conducive to his work style. Fortunately, we went back to the drawing board, spending much more time in defining the culture that was present at the company. The next candidate we placed is still there today.

Three Reasons to Institute an Onboarding Process

1. Onboarding helps new hires feel that they are part of a larger organization and that they are important.

2. Onboarding helps align the new hire with the corporate culture of the organization.
3. Onboarding expedites the learning curve—helping to get new hires up to speed and productive.

Effective Onboarding Programs

First, effective onboarding programs engage the new employee. Some companies even manage to make them fun. For instance, one of my clients uses a scavenger hunt format for employee orientation. The new employees are charged with collecting items from around the company. Filling out tax forms, finding the vending machine in the break room, reading the company mission—all items collected in scavenger hunt format.

Many companies use the Internet to engage their new employees in the onboarding process. Employees visit a site where they are provided with corporate history, values, strategy, and fiscal goals. Video technology has helped make these presentations personal. For example, online videos can be used to provide an overview of the finances conducted by the chief financial officer (CFO), and a greeting from a senior-level executive. I've even seen video office tours narrated by an employee.

Second, good onboarding programs include **short-term, midterm, and long-term strategies.** Short-term strategies include intensive one- to two-day sessions to orient the new employee. Midterm strategies include 30- and 60-day reviews, rotational assignments, and special projects that are designed to expose the new employee to parts of the company they would not normally have contact with. Long-term strategies include annual reviews, continuing education plans, and career goal setting. The most effective long-term strategy is mentorship. Research shows that providing a mentor is a major contributor to increased productivity and lower turnover.

The third component of an effective onboarding program is the inclusion of the new employee's direct manager in the onboarding process. Some firms provide "new manager training" in order to address this component. Other strategies include team-building exercises or luncheons designed exclusively for managers and their new hires. The key is to ensure that the direct manager has ownership in their new employee's onboarding process.

The Three Phases of the Onboarding Program

1. **Short term.** Conduct your company's standard training, which includes your company overview, policies and procedures, projects, introductions, and the like. Spend two weeks of intense training, and then hand over the reins.
2. **Medium term.** Remember those skills gaps you identified during the interview process? Make a plan to address those shortcomings with additional training, especially in the area of technical skills.
3. **Long term.** Designed to address employee orientation over the life cycle of their career, long-term onboarding programs focus on creating deep roots within an organization. Career growth, corporate politics, and corporate communications are explored over years of development.

Onboarding, done properly, will help bring a new employee up to speed quickly, while at the same time setting them up for long-term success.

Onboarding's Increased Importance

During rocky economic times onboarding takes on new importance. It is critical to ensure that those people you have spent so much time attracting and aligning with your organization stay with you. Employees who go through an onboarding process feel better connected to their colleagues and to the company culture. This translates into improved retention rates. Onboarding in tough economic times becomes a critical tool for success.

Here is a short onboarding checklist. See Appendix IV for a more detailed sample.

Onboarding Checklist Sample 1

Department/Payroll Info

- W-4 federal form completed and sent to Payroll.
- W-4 state form completed and sent to Payroll.
- Patent policy form.
- Conflict-of-interest policy statement.
- Ensure that employee has accessed the internal directory to confirm personal data and to provide emergency notification contact.
- Confirm with employee the name and phone number of employee relations representative.

Human Resources

- Complete I-9.
- Complete conflict-of-interest employment form.
- ID number issued by human resources.
- New employee orientation scheduled by HR for _____.

Access Information

- Establish email account.
- Establish access to appropriate computer files.
- Provide access to company intranet.
- Issue passwords.
- Establish phone extension.
- Activate voice mail.
- Provide long distance access code.
- Add employee's name to any email group lists, distribution lists, internal/office phone lists, and/or web site.

Departmental Orientation and Office Access

- Inform staff of employee's arrival.
- Set up and clean office space.
- Obtain office supplies.

- Establish training schedule.
- Establish office mailbox.
- Introduce employee to staff on first day. Bring on tour of building/ office/facilities including lunchroom, emergency exits, and restrooms.
- Indicate location of parking lot/rapid transit station.
- Provide keys (office, building, desk, file cabinets, etc.).
- Provide security codes if necessary.
- Show location of fax machines, copiers, printers, and the like; provide instruction and any access information.
- Review dress code and office protocol.
- Explain completion of time sheet.
- Review pay schedule.
- Confirm work schedule.

Relevant Work-Related Items

- Business cards ordered.
- Nameplates ordered.
- Name badge issued.
- Pay card issued.
- Cell phone policy covered.
- PDA policy covered.
- Laptop issued.
- Manuals/handbooks supplied.
- Other: _____

MATCH

The Process:
Phase IV

Following Up

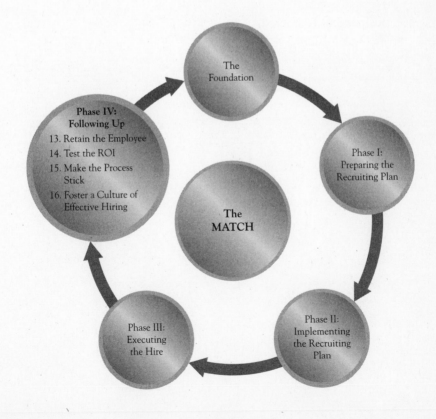

Thought you were done with the MATCH process once you onboarded your new employee? Well, not quite. After all the hard work involved in hiring the right person, you must now concern yourself with retention. Further, now is the time for the hiring team to reflect on the process itself, to understand what went right and what things could be improved upon. MATCH is ultimately about changing your organization's *culture* and establishing the ongoing search for talented people into the fabric of your existence. This final phase questions your return on investment (ROI), makes the process stick, and produces a feedback loop that fosters a culture of effective hiring.

Retain the Employee

Step 13

Coming together is a beginning. Keeping together is progress. Working together is success.

—Henry Ford

C ongratulations! Your company has a new person to contribute to its success. This person has been thoughtfully considered and interviewed. They have even been through an onboarding process and assigned a mentor. Both you and the new employee are excited about the future.

So how are you going to retain them? Though that might seem like an odd question to consider before they even get settled into their space, that's exactly the point: you need to be thinking about how you will keep your employees *before* they walk through the door.

The reality is that by going through the MATCH process you have already greatly increased the odds of retaining talent. After all, capturing the heart of an employee by aligning them with the overall purpose of the organization and then clearly defining what they will be accountable for is a terrific way to start the relationship. If you have followed each step of the MATCH process, then your hire will already deeply connect to your company.

Sticky Notes:

- Retention strategies start with the mission of your organization.

- Improve retention by understanding generational differences.

- A solid mentoring program is the most effective retention strategy.

But you can even further impact retention by developing an understanding of what continuously motivates people about their work. Part of the retention conundrum is answered by looking several years down the road. It's equally important to know what hinders that motivation and prompts productive, energetic, and creative people to leave a company.

Top performers essentially want three things:

- A compelling opportunity to use and grow their talents
- Appreciation from a company with a strong vision
- Leadership they can respect and learn from

This last point is particularly important. We've noted that a person does not quit a company. He or she quits a boss or a department. Most morale problems don't happen at a systemic level; they take place within departments and among individuals, when workers lose their focus on producing value for others and instead start focusing on—well, *anything* else. Therefore, one of the most critical things you can do for retention is to continually cultivate your managers. Managers must know, believe in, and embody the company's mission. That's where it all starts. Keep them growing, especially in the areas of communications, project planning and execution, and you'll see retention increase as a result.

First, Understand Your Own Framework

Over the past decade the workplace has changed drastically in *how* we do work, as well as our attitudes about both our tasks and the workplace itself. While it's natural to feel that your particular generation has the right approach to work, it's also counterproductive. A better approach is to understand how others see things before trying to impose your framework on them. Generational gaps are most acute between the Baby Boomers (those born between 1944 and 1964), and the latter generations (Gen X, Gen Y). Generalizing about these two groups is a bit hazardous and unfair, but the broad truths are nonetheless a driving force in the workplace:

- **Baby Boomers work to "belong."** Their jobs give them a certain sense of identity; not only their titles, but the companies for which they work, as in, "I'm vice president of sales for X company." Baby Boomers want to cultivate a sense of connection to an organization. They are loyal to the hierarchy and willing to do what the boss says. In exchange for that loyalty, they expect job security. When they have that, they will tough out any work assignment and stay until the job is done. At the same time, their "work" life is sharply demarcated from their "personal" lives. Baby Boomers are not interested in integrating these two aspects of their existence, nor do they particularly need to find fun and personal fulfillment at work. Many of them don't even care for praise. They get a paycheck and advancement; that's their reward. "Work is called 'work' for a reason," one manager told me. "It's not supposed to be fun."
- **Generation X and later**, however, comfortably blend their personal and work lives. They're at ease working within a flat organization, provided they're engaged in fun and interesting projects. They're built to work in teams, and after work they enjoy hanging out with their friends from (where else?) work. They're interested in what a company does socially—parties, bowling, playing softball, and so on. They also spend time volunteering, and care about a company's values and social conscience. Even if they're not the decision makers themselves, they expect higher-ups to consider their opinions and are not shy about expressing them. In school, this generation was constantly rewarded for small accomplishments, and they expect management to acknowledge the steps of their progress as well as their outcomes. "If there is extra work to be done, I'll do it, but probably from home and/or on the weekends," a young manager once told me.

The inherent conflicts in these two approaches to work are obvious: some Baby Boomers see the Gen X crowd as too casual, a little lazy and self-absorbed, and not tough enough for extended challenges.

Some Gen Xers see the Baby Boomers as slow, rigid in their thinking, and in need of a "real life." They can't imagine being defined by one's work, or even being particularly loyal to one company.

Neither group is right or wrong; each has its own strengths and shortcomings. The point here is to simply acknowledge that you do *have* a certain framework through which you view the world—whether you realize this or not—but that the framework is not an absolute reality; it's just *your* reality. Noting your own tendencies and making some accommodations can greatly help you as a first step in managing your retention.

The Retention Areas

What follows is a list of the five key areas that are critical for keeping employees on board.

1. **A clear mission and purpose.** People want to be part of an organization that they can be proud of. They also want clarity on what their organization does and how they do it.
2. **Flexibility.** Flexibility rules in today's workplace. One-size-fits-all approaches have lost their effectiveness in our demanding and diverse world.
3. **Open communication.** In this era of ubiquitous technology, people have come to expect instant information. High-retention workplaces make it a priority to ensure open lines of communication. Intranets, weekly emails from the leadership team, and even internal blogs have helped to address this need for communication.
4. **Reward and recognition.** All humans need to feel appreciated; reward and recognition programs help meet that need. These must be "from the heart"; today's employees will quickly see through shallow pats on the back.
5. **Training and development.** Employees want an opportunity to grow. Providing a path for development of skills and potential will enhance their ability to contribute, while increasing odds of retention.

Mentoring

We covered mentoring in the precious chapter on onboarding. But as a critical retention strategy, it is worth mentioning in the chapter at hand. Mentoring is both a key to integrating an employee to a new company and an excellent way to retain that employee.

Virtually every executive I've ever spoken to credits their ascension through the ranks to the assistance they received from mentors. Some participated in formal mentoring programs, while others simply had a series of informal mentors. Some mentors helped employees develop their skills; others guided them through the company's culture; others went to bat for them at critical milestones in their careers; and others just gave them a variety of personal and professional advice. In every case, however, the mentor helped their mentee grow and—perhaps even more importantly—helped them cultivate a strong bond with the company. There is nothing like that sense of connection to keep employees happy and retention high.

Retention Strategies

In this chapter we've explored the utilization of several methods for improving retention. Here are a few more very specific retention strategies:

- **Training.** Training on skills is a good place to start with new employees. During the interview process, you noted certain areas where the employee fell short. Be honest with the employee; let him or her know about the areas in which you believe they need to grow. Develop a training program you both agree on. If the issue is, say, one of management experience, agree to work with the employee to aid him or her in gaining that experience.
- **One-on-one meetings.** Arrange a series of one-on-one meetings to establish personal relationships. Understanding the generational frameworks is important here, as is good management

and mentoring. You want to get the employee contributing, connecting, and growing right from the start.

- **Involve the new hire with the next hire.** Get the new hire involved with the next hire you make. There is no experience quite like being on the hiring team to make one feel connected to the organization. In addition, this new member will have some unique and fresh insights into your process, having just been on the receiving side.

- **Ask the hiring team.** Focusing on the issue of retention with your hiring team will produce a number of workable and innovative strategies specific to your company. That's a great thing!

- **Be proactive.** You don't want to be in the position of developing a retention strategy as a reaction to a person or group of people leaving on poor terms. It's far better to address retention strategies as part of your hiring process.

Test the Return on Investment

Step 14

It has been my experience that competency in mathematics, both in numerical manipulations and in understanding its conceptual founda-tions, enhances a person's ability to handle the more ambiguous and qualitative relationships that dominate our day-to-day financial decision making.

—Alan Greenspan

People have a natural aversion to any exercise that attempts to express human behavior in terms of numbers. This is especially true when you try to quantify the impact the employee has on an organization. You can almost hear rock singer Bob Seger in the background screaming, "I feel like a number! I'm not a number!"

At the simplest level, for-profit organizations survive on the ability to make more money than they spend. Nonprofits differ in that they must satisfy their mission without exceeding their capital resources. As such, all organizations must (at some level) compare the costs of a hire with the value of the employee's contributions. There is nothing new here, though it often seems forgotten that long-term survival is based upon allocating people resources in such a way as to ensure that more money is coming in than is going out.

Sticky Notes:

- Create a system for evaluating hiring ROI.

- Hiring ROI can be measured by calculating and avoiding the cost of a mishire, increased revenue/efficiency, and measuring the cultural impact.

- Challenge your organization to question and improve your hiring ROI.

Evaluating hiring return on investment (ROI) recognizes the fine art of balancing human capital measurement with proper respect for the individual. Three areas that can be measured are:

1. **Calculating and avoiding the cost of a mishire**—not an actual increase in revenue or efficiency, but saving money by avoiding the wrong hire.
2. **Increased revenue/efficiency**—measurable bottom-line increases that are directly tied to the work of the new hire.
3. **Cultural impact**—the positive influence on the culture or spirit of the organization.

Calculating and Avoiding the Cost of a Mishire

Check out Appendix III, "The Cost of a Mishire: The Story of the Bad Controller." I won't spoil the plot by telling you how much this controller cost the company, but I think you will be astounded. Even with these dramatic costs, I've even been told by many that my estimated costs are conservative.

After all, consider the areas that are affected by a mishire:

Hiring	Compensation	Maintenance	Severence
• Recruitment/ search fee	• Base salary	• Administrative assistant	• Severance fee
• Outside testing	• Bonuses for all years	• Office rental	• Outplacement counseling fee
• HR department time	• Stock options	• Furniture, computer, etc.	• Costs in negotiating separation
• HR department administration	• Benefits	• Travel (air, food, lodging)	• Costs in lawsuits
• Travel costs	• Clubs/ organizations	• Training	• Administrative costs
• Time expenses for non-HR personnel			• Wasted time
• Relocation fees			• "Bad press"

And those hard costs don't even address the mistakes, failures, and missed or wasted business opportunities:

- What if the mishire hired others? Are *they* potential mishires, too?
- What about impaired customer loyalty; failure to enter a new, hot market; wasted money on poor software decisions; and launching "dog" projects?

Occasionally when I walk clients through the MATCH process, their reaction is, "Wow, looks painful." They see all the steps and little details that one must attend to and wonder if they have enough time, resources, and energy to work the process correctly. But the fact is, if you hurry the process and don't hire correctly the first time, you're just going to have to do it again and again—until you either get very lucky or learn your lesson. And in the meantime, you'll be draining your company not only of money, but also morale.

Analyzing Increased Revenue/Efficiency

Increased revenue is the easiest way to measure hiring ROI. The impact of a new hire can be calculated by establishing an objective measurable baseline and then noting bottom-line improvements over time. This is easy to analyze when you've hired a salesperson or an executive with leadership responsibilities, more difficult when reviewing results achieved by an accountant, or an administrative assistant, or an information technology (IT) manager. However, both the company and the employee benefit by evaluating the ROI of every hire.

Revenue per Employee (RPE)

A simple way to establish a baseline is through the concept of revenue per employee (RPE). RPE can be calculated with the following simple formula:

$$\frac{\text{Revenue of the company}}{\text{Number of employees}}$$

Suppose that a company of 312 employees has revenues of $50 million. You calculate RPE by dividing $50 million by 312, which is $160,256. This figure then becomes the baseline for evaluating the impact of a new hire. Companies can improve RPE by either increasing revenue or decreasing the number of employees (thereby increasing efficiency). Following are three real-life instances where nonmanagers were tasked with impacting the RPE and how the impact was measured.

Web Site Developer

By improving an existing web site, the web site developer was able to increase traffic, directly affecting return traffic and time on site. These metrics were compared to a baseline taken on the web site developer's start date and compared on a quarterly basis. The most critical metric for evaluating the web developer's ROI was increased sales through the web site improvements. Complications did arise because the improvement of the web site was shared by the marketing team, and sales were impacted by the sales team; however, there was a clear correlation to the web improvements and increased sales, which impacted the RPE and therefore the hiring ROI.

Database Manager

By setting a goal of decreasing the number of bad emails in an email marketing campaign, the database manager was able to increase the number of sales leads, which led to one additional sale per quarter. By tracking sales leads that came from emails, which had been corrected through a research process, the database manager was able to correlate an improved RPE to her direct actions.

Office Manager

Collections were not a priority when the office manager joined the company. Sales were good, but there was not enough money in the bank. The office manager was tasked with reducing the number of Days Sales Outstanding (DSO). By improving the collections process the office manager was able to clearly establish an excellent ROI by directly affecting the cash accessible at any given time— this in turn affected the overall RPE of the company.

Cultural Impact

The most difficult area to measure is the influence that a new hire has on the organization's culture. I'll turn to sports to illustrate a positive correlation. In 1995, my hometown baseball team the

Atlanta Braves, were struggling. To try to turn things around, they brought in a veteran first baseman named Fred McGriff.

A fire broke out in the clubhouse the day McGriff joined the team—which turned out to be a metaphor for how McGriff would help to ignite the Braves. His mature, self-effacing, quiet style seemed to be just what the team needed. The more they won, the bigger each game got; and the bigger the game, the more pressure the team faced. McGriff's easy going personality helped the team stay relaxed and focused even as the intensity of their circumstances increased. The Braves went on to win not only the division, but also the World Series.

McGriff didn't win games single-handedly, of course. Though he played very well, it wasn't just his ability that clinched the championship for the Braves. It was how the rest of the team responded to his presence. Truly, his impact couldn't be calculated with runs batted in, home runs, or any other statistic. But the effect that McGriff had on the Braves organization is undeniable.

Organizations must strive in a similar way to understand the impact that employees have on company morale and spirit. I've seen several great companies who have linchpins like Fred McGriff in every position—from administrative assistants to presidents and CEOs. While company leaders must have the capacity to transform the organization, don't underestimate or ignore the capacity of *every* team member to create a positive cultural dynamic.

To measure this cultural dynamic, the hiring team should challenge themselves to discuss the impact of the new employee. In follow-up meetings, the team should question the effect that the new hire has had on the team. While this is a very difficult area to directly measure, discussion on the topic will help the organization to better understand the importance of this aspect of hiring ROI.

In addition, you might wish to survey your employees on their job satisfaction once a year and compare results from quarter to quarter. As we discussed in the chapter on retention, workers who feel good about their work are more likely to offer their creativity— which, in the knowledge economy, translates directly to competitive advantage.

The Best Candidate Available for the Money

There's one more concept to keep in mind as you are working to establish hiring ROI: hiring the best candidate available for the money. Unless you have unlimited funds, you will almost always have to compromise your search. So understand that the "right" hire isn't simply the best candidate out there; it's the best person available for the salary you can afford.

If you are a small company, you likely cannot employ a controller at a price tag of $200,000 annually. Your perfect controller may be at $75,000—certainly a different set of skills, experiences, and image, but nonetheless, the right controller for you at this time.

Should your company grow, the controller who was the right fit at one time may no longer be capable of the job. At that point, the organization will have to conduct a new search for the best candidate available for the money.

Measuring ROI

I was recently impressed by a story in which an analyst developed a process that allowed her organization to use Excel in streamlining a process. This improvement took a three-day ordeal and compressed it to less than five minutes. The employee's manager calculated the hourly savings to the company and gave her a spot bonus based on a percentage of the savings.

Certainly, I was impressed with this analyst's creativity and know-how. But I was further impressed that her company recognized the contribution and quickly compensated inventive thinking. It is no surprise that her company is wildly successful. By consistently recognizing and appreciating innovative ways to save money, the company is developing a culture of ROI appreciation.

How can you instill a greater appreciation of ROI in your company?

Make the Process Stick

Step 15

Champions keep playing until they get it right.

—Billie Jean King

remember first being exposed to the steps of the scientific method in middle school:

1. Ask a question.
2. Do background research.
3. Form a hypothesis.
4. Test the hypothesis by performing an experiment.
5. Analyze the data.
6. Draw a conclusion.
7. If the hypothesis is true, report results. But if the hypothesis is false or only partially true, then go back and construct a new hypothesis.

Sticky Notes:

- Evaluate your hiring process like a scientist conducting an experiment.

- Ask new hires how you could improve the process.

- Schedule a debrief session to plan, do, observe, and reflect.

In the eighth grade, we used the scientific method to determine if a plant in the closet grew faster than one in the sun, or if warm tennis balls bounced higher than cold tennis balls. The MATCH process uses the same scientific approach to improve hiring within your company. When you achieve a successful result, the process is designed to retain the steps that proved effective; and when your results are less than successful the process is designed to isolate and improve upon those steps. Let's follow through with the analogy, so we can make hiring the right person a cornerstone of your company.

1. **Ask a question.** Throughout this book, I have asserted that the company mission should drive a hire. What compelling reason does a company have to hire? Why should a company commit resources to a hire? The answer must stem from the purpose or mission of the company's existence. For our science projects, we asked, "Which will boil faster, hot or cold water?" For our companies, our question should be, "Will hiring an employee at this cost with these skills and this personality better allow us to profitably achieve our mission?"

2. **Do background research.** In middle school, we went to the library and wrote down pertinent information from the encyclopedia. In MATCH, we assemble the hiring team, clarify the corporate culture, create the org chart, compile a job overview, create the competency profile, develop the recruiting plan, conduct the phone screen, conduct behavioral face-to-face interviews, conduct behavioral reference checks, complete background checks, etc. These steps constitute a research-based approach to evaluating the candidate that will best align with our business objective.

3. **Form a hypothesis.** An educated guess: the warm tennis balls will bounce higher than the cold tennis balls, the plant kept in the closet will not grow as tall as the plant kept in the sunlight, and cold water will boil faster than warm water. An educated guess in hiring is "Candidate X will bring our organization more value than Candidates A, B, or C." While MATCH is designed to take the guess work out of the process, let's face it—at the intersection of making the decision, extending the offer, and receiving acceptance, you are incapable of knowing with 100 percent certainty how a candidate will perform.

4. **Test the hypothesis by performing an experiment.** Ovens, freezers, thermometers, measuring tape, and so on were the tools we used in our school projects. The test for the hypothesis in the art of business is the bottom line—or in bigger organizations, specific business objectives that tie back to the organizational

mission. Just as when we were in school, businesses should make the objectives of the hire quantifiable. Further, the company should strive to keep all variables constant except that being observed. This is equally difficult to do in both science and business. However, it is critical to the validity of the experiment/hire in both cases to objectively observe the cause-and-effect impact at its most fundamental level.

5. **Analyze the data.** "The warm tennis balls bounced (on average) 5.4 inches higher than the cold tennis balls when dropped from 24 inches above the concrete floor." "The median height of the plant in the closet was 3.6 inches shorter than the plant in the sunlight after 21 days." "The cold water's mean boiling time was 9.6 minutes; while the hot water's mean boiling time was 8.9 minutes." Similarly, throughout the MATCH process, I advocate testing the hiring ROI: objectively observing the value that the hire is bringing to the business equation.

6. **Draw a conclusion.** Our hypothesis was correct: "warm tennis balls *do* bounce higher than cold tennis balls." "Plants kept in closets don't grow as well as the plants kept in the sun" (no surprise there, I hope). But in direct contradiction to old wives' tales—though not the laws of physics—"hot water boils more quickly than does cold water." In business, the critical step of evaluating the new hire is contained in the question: is the individual exceeding the criteria for success?

7. **If the hypothesis is true, report results, but if the hypothesis is false or partially true, then go back and construct a new hypothesis.** This was my favorite part of the scientific method. I thought it was cool that if your hypothesis proved wrong, you could follow the arrow on the diagram back to the formulation of the hypothesis and restart. How great is that—a scientific reset button. In school, we reformulated our assumption that cold water boiled faster than hot water, and then confirmed that hypothesis with a new set of experiments, which showed that, in fact, hot water boiled an average of 0.7 minutes faster than cold water. We must do the same thing in business. I don't know how many times I have heard successful professionals tell me that the only reason for their success was trying, trying, and trying again, with no concern for failure. What others label a

"failure," successful people call a "learning experience." When something didn't work, they'd cast it aside; when something did work, they repeated the behavior. No great genius was needed—just persistence and attention to results. Hence, that is the idea behind this chapter: make the process stick.

Let's examine efforts needed to create this scientific climate:

Making the Right Process Stick

The MATCH process is a systematic approach to hiring and retaining the *right* person. Therefore, once we have hired the person, we must continue evaluating the process itself. A constant system of self-checking will allow the process to grow and adapt to changes. In over 10 years as an executive recruiter, I've seen hiring markets change almost overnight. For that reason, the MATCH process must constantly evolve. While fundamentals remain intact, techniques within the system will have to adapt.

In order to create a living and learning hiring process, the hiring team must remain vigilant. An objective meeting immediately following the initiation of the new hire is a must. But further, I suggest that that the hiring team meet at the three-month and one-year marks in order to summarily review the entire MATCH process (from inception to retention). Again, a culture of communication must be fostered. Congratulations should be in order, but dig deeply into any areas that could have made the hire more effective.

The Feedback Loop

By utilizing a disciplined approach to reviewing the MATCH process, the hiring team will create a feedback loop. Areas of noted improvement will enhance the next hiring effort, and discovered pitfalls will be avoided. Again, note that this process must be carefully documented in order to maximize the effect. It doesn't matter what the hiring team learns if there is no way to communicate the learning.

The question that I get most often in regards to this feedback loop is: "If our organization hires a certain position (like a controller) only once every decade, then isn't creating a feedback loop a waste of time?" My answer is no; but be rational about the process. Simply create a controller file in a place you'll be able to access. Here, you'll store the job overview, competencies, behavioral questions, résumés of candidates not chosen, notes from the meetings, and any other pertinent information (you'll want to include notes from reviews as well). By deploying the resources necessary for finalizing the process in this way, you will save a great deal of time over the life span of your organization.

Be sure to include the new hire in the evaluative process. Not only can you learn from his or her perspective, but you can also start to share the culture that supports a systematic hiring process. Ask the new hire what they liked and disliked about the process. Find out what attracted them to the role. Ask for suggestions to improve the process. Be sure to record this information so that the hiring team can evaluate potential areas of improvement.

Since **feedback** is a circular process whereby some proportion of a system's output is returned (fed back) to the input, data must be collected and analyzed at the end of every hire in order to enhance the overall process. Investigating the following areas can significantly improve the value of the feedback loop:

- **The hiring team.** Did the hiring team stay constant throughout the process? Was it necessary to add or subtract from the group? What could you do to improve the group dynamics?
- **Clarifying the corporate culture.** Does your corporate culture document accurately match your organization's actual culture? Were you able to more clearly identify your company's identity through the process?
- **The organization chart.** What revisions do you need to make to the org chart reflecting the recent hire or other changes in the company?
- **The job overview.** Were any changes made to the job overview? Keeping the job overview on file for future hires can save the company time, money, and energy. Also, keeping notes from the job interview process can help in managing the employee. In fact, continued reference to the job overview during the employee's tenure can further help to establish an excellent resource for continued growth and improvement.

- **The competency profile.** Were your priorities indeed the most critical aspects of the hire? Was the team objective enough, or did they create a competency based on subjectivity? Did the competencies outlined match the business goals that are to be performed by the employee?
- **The recruiting plan.** Did the plan effectively produce the "right" candidate? Should other sources be considered in the future? Could the company find the right talent for less money, or does the budget need to be increased?
- **Implementing the recruiting plan.** Could the behavioral questions be improved? What improvements could be implemented and used for the next hire? Did the team discover any "holes" when comparing candidates' responses with their references' responses? Should you add any additional background checks?
- **Executing the hire.** Was your job offer accepted without negotiation? Was the candidate counteroffered, and what was the reaction? How quickly did the candidate acclimate to the team?
- **Following up.** Is the employee still with the company? Is he or she productive and bringing value to the organization? Is the employee helping others to achieve more? And, finally, are we creating a better hiring environment by asking these very questions?

A Suggested Format Is the Debrief Session

The purpose of a debrief session is to improve the hiring process by capturing the lessons learned and making them *explicit*; that is, recording them (generally in a document) and then working them into the process for the next hire.

In the Army, these debrief sessions are called "After Action Reviews" (AARs). The rules of an AAR as applied to business are:

- It does not judge success or failure.
- It attempts to discover why things happened.
- It focuses directly on the tasks and goals that were to be accomplished.
- It encourages employees to surface important lessons in the discussion.

Your debrief session should be facilitated by human resources (HR) and include all who were involved in the hiring process (except the candidate.) An administrator should take notes. You can use the flowchart in this book to complete the hiring steps and tell the story of the hire. Make sure that all involved have a chance to comment on each of the steps. You may find that, for instance, while your interview went very well, another interviewer felt unprepared to talk to the candidate. Focus on the process—did the unprepared interviewer not get the materials in time? Was the person properly trained in interviewing techniques?

As you examine the story of the hire, take time to note the things that went particularly well. Not only does this help you feel good about the process, it reinforces those actions for the group. Analyze the process for areas that did not work as well because, in most cases, mistakes are a result of not following procedure. Did you skip steps? If so, why? Note the areas for improvement and action steps necessary to address those issues for future interviews. Make sure that HR acts as the keeper of these action steps.

The AARs look at a continual cycle of "Plan, Do, Observe, Reflect," and the interview process can be examined in the same way. Unfortunately, many companies neglect the "Observe" and "Reflect" phases of the process, and subsequently repeat the same mistakes.

The end product of your review should be a bulleted list of lessons learned that you can use for the next round of hiring. Make these points action oriented, such as:

- Use a quieter conference room on other side of the building for interviews.
- Have HR do mock interview sessions with new interviewers before they see the candidate.
- Make sure *all* notes are turned in the day of the interviews—no exceptions!
- Do a group interview for technical skills.

You should go over this list the next time you assemble the hiring team for another hire. Build on the list. Refine it. And incorporate it into your hiring approach. That's how you make the process stick.

Foster a Culture of Effective Hiring

Step 16

Excellence is an art won by training and habituation. We do not act rightly because we have virtue or excellence, but we rather have those because we have acted rightly. We are what we repeatedly do. Excellence, then, is not an act but a habit.

—Aristotle

Have you ever had problems establishing a new habit? Perhaps the better question is, have you ever *not* had a problem establishing a new habit? Whether it is becoming more organized, eating less, learning a musical instrument, writing in a journal—establishing a new habit is excruciatingly difficult. But, have you noticed that once you've gone through the difficult process of establishing a routine, it becomes easier to maintain?

Let's use exercising as an example. Most people find that exercising every day is easier than exercising only once or twice a week. Establishing a pattern makes the exercise event easier over time. Soon, the pattern becomes a habit, the habit becomes a culture—and once established as a culture, it is very difficult to break.

Personally, I discovered this human characteristic when studying for my college classes. I found it much easier to hit the books every night than every once in a while. By making the process of nightly studying a habit, opening the books became a painless undertaking—a natural act instead of an accomplishment.

Sticky Notes:

- The business leader should strive to make effective hiring an organizational habit.

- Work on establishing small consistent changes as you establish a new culture.

- … and back to the mission.

MATCH is intended to establish hiring process habits in a similar way—habits that will hopefully become an integral part of your organization's culture.

Before you can begin habitualizing hiring best practices, there are two critical elements that must be in place.

1. **The culture of effective hiring must start at the top of the organization.** In fact, this is the heart of leadership—establishing culture. Great leaders don't dictate; they develop community around concepts. To create a culture of effective hiring, the rallying cry must be around the hiring process.

   Note: I am often asked, "What if my organization does not care about hiring the right people? Can I facilitate change?" The answer is an infuriating "maybe."

   I have seen nonrecognized leaders experience great fulfillment by helping recognized leadership teams create a culture of effective hiring. It is not surprising that the instigator of the movement to create a culture of effective hiring often finds themselves quickly promoted to a role of recognized leader.

   The other result, which I have seen as well, is that the instigator either leaves or is asked to leave the company. In both cases, I believe that the individual will find him- or herself in a better spot.

2. **The culture of effective hiring must always map back to the mission.** A flimsy or superficial mission will not stimulate the best and the brightest; nor will tomorrow's leaders be inspired by a "flavor of the day" approach to creating a culture of hiring. The movement must be authentic or it will fail. The organization's mission must transparently act as the cornerstone of its culture. The cause must be the mission, with the effect being an appropriate hire—and that cause and effect model must be clear to all.

Foster a Culture of Effective Hiring

The Japanese philosophy kaizen gives us an excellent model to utilize as we attempt to foster a culture of effective hiring. *Kaizen* focuses on continuous but small change. The person who introduced me to kaizen suggested that organizational change is akin to changing the course of an ocean liner. As with an ocean liner, there are no shortcuts in establishing a culture of effective hiring.

We live in an impatient world. We want change overnight, but rarely is the human organism capable of such immediate change. Though we might be able to discipline ourselves for a short period, we often revert to our previous behavior. To change culture we must think of our company as that ocean liner, making slow and steady process toward the goal of a culture that celebrates the exceptional hire.

The kaizen approach can be represented in the story of an individual who wants to wake up an hour earlier. Instead of going "cold turkey" and setting the alarm an hour earlier, kaizen would have the early riser get up a minute earlier for 60 days. The belief is that bodies adapt better to slow and steady change. Just as this works with individuals looking to change their habits, the philosophy of kaizen has been applied by very successful corporations. In fact, Toyota counts kaizen as one of the cornerstones of its success.

I am not suggesting here that you imitate Toyota by implementing a kaizen program. My point is simply to encourage you to go slow and steady as you attempt to make systemic changes.

Creating a Culture of Continuous Improvement in the Area of Hiring

Culture is not something that you can buy or a goal that can be attained. It is truly never finished. Culture must be contemplated, focused on, prodded, and discussed—with passionate fanaticism—*always*. My dad, Bert Erling, always told me, "Being unsatisfied is a good thing." And as is often the case, my dad was right.

No organization ever "arrives" at an effective hiring culture. There are too many moving parts for us to rest on our laurels. Economic changes, hiring patterns, social trends, and more create an ever changing world that requires extraordinary focus in order to stay competitive. However, the MATCH process offers a systematic approach for constantly pushing hiring culture onto your organizational radar screen.

You can focus on a culture of hiring excellence by establishing and maintaining a monthly or quarterly checkup. This should not be a session where the leadership team gets together and talks about specific hiring issues; in fact, every attempt should be made to avoid specifics. Rather, these meetings should be philosophical discussions that might include topics such as:

- What are we doing to attract the best talent?
- Are we communicating our need for talent to each member of our team? What could we do better in this arena?
- What is our competition doing to attract talent?
- Who have we lost recently? How could this loss have been avoided (if at all)?
- Are we constantly improving our hiring process?
- Are we gaining insight from our feedback loop?
- Are we making progress in establishing a culture of effective hiring?

On and on, and on and on. . . .

The process of reflection—of returning some portion of the output to the input of the system—must be done over and over again. Over time, the organization chart, the corporate culture, the job descriptions, the competency profile, and the like will become more and more refined. This will create a culture where the right person will be hired increasingly more often.

The Mission Still Drives the Hire

We started with the mission, and we end with the mission. Through the MATCH process employees of the organization gain ownership and align intrinsically with the company's mission. As you move through the steps of this methodology, not only are you improving the odds of hiring the right person every time, but you are also strengthening your team. Using the MATCH process brings everyone together around the values of your organization.

CONCLUSION

So What Does MATCH Stand For?

For those of you follow my blog, you may recall that the original, working title for this book was *Mission Critical Hiring, or "MCH."* Early on, I liked the title because, as I've shown, working from a mission is, well, *critical* to hiring. Plus, I thought the play on words was rather clever.

As the book took its final form, however, it was clear that the original title did not encompass the whole of the process. I needed something "broader," and of course my publisher wanted a title with some zing. Still, I couldn't quite let go of *Mission Critical Hiring.* After all, it had been the working title for more than two years. We went back and forth with several names. We settled on MATCH, which I am very pleased with on a number of levels, not the least of which was because it retained my M, C, and H—and in the same order!

MATCH forces us to focus on that which is crucial. In creating a thriving organization, we can take shortcuts in some areas, but not in the area of hiring people. Peter Drucker told us to "focus on first things first, and second things not at all." The MATCH process forces us to focus on the most critical aspect of hiring, aligning the right person with the right job.

This book originated in the act of compiling hiring best practices for my recruiting firm. With year after year of stellar results, our clients began to ask how we were doing this. I started to share our techniques, encouraging companies to create a systematic approach to hiring around their missions. Over time, my collection of best practices began to resemble a book. Many sleep-deprived nights later, I was able to produce the book you have in hand.

Doubtless, as I continue to talk about hiring, I will refine concepts (in fact, I encourage you to dialogue with me and others on my blog at www.danerling.com). However, the fundamentals of the hiring process will never change. In my research and hands-on-experience, I have found that the process outlined in this book works today, it would have worked 100 years ago, and it will work 100 years from now. The fundamental principles are timeless.

I hope the ideas, techniques, and materials in this book bring you value. It would please me greatly to hear that your company was more profitable by implementing the MATCH process. But an even greater sense of accomplishment would be to know that not only was the company able to achieve better financial results, but that bottom-line improvement coincided with a clearer sense of purpose and a stronger set of values.

Idealism doesn't belong in business. Brutal realities must be the main concern of those running a profitable company—no rose colored glasses allowed. But that does not mean that you can't have a mission. In fact, a sense of mission becomes more and more tantamount in attracting those people who can help to carry the company toward profitability. The workforce of today and of the future wants to clearly understand and derive meaning from their careers. They care about values—it is not just about the bottom line any more.

By utilizing MATCH, companies will develop a culture around their mission. From the decision to make a hire to the decision on who to hire, mission plays a vital role. And not only will the new hire understand the mission of the organization, but all those on the hiring team will be reminded of the purpose and values for which the company exists.

A View from Inside a Recruiting Firm

As the president of a recruiting firm, occasionally I find myself conflicted when a customer has no interest in a process-oriented approach to hiring. For instance, our firm recently got a call from a business owner who "wanted a senior accountant—yesterday." This business owner didn't have time to give us a good job description, nor did he have time to meet us, and when we asked for 30 minutes to discuss competencies, he became perturbed.

What this business owner doesn't understand is that by treating a recruiting firm like a commodity, he puts himself at a disadvantage. Internally, we put a job like this in the "C-level" file. We may send a few résumés, but there's not much value we can offer. It isn't that we want to behave in this way, but there are other clients who have committed to us, and those clients get our attention first. And by the way, we certainly do try to inform the client of the position he is putting himself in—if he will listen.

Further, what this business owner doesn't understand is that trying to rush a senior accountant hire (or any hire for that matter) is almost always a mistake. How frustrating that we have a systematic proven process that nearly ensures that the business owner *will* hire the right candidate, but the hiring manager will not take the two hours of time on the front end of the search, taking care to align with a good recruiting firm, and compiling a careful profile and job description. So the result is that to avoid two hours of work, countless time, energy, and money are risked in a careless hiring process.

By the way, there are occasions where a company must get help quickly. In cases where an employee gets ill or other unexpected circumstances arise, then there is not always time to do a thorough search. When this happens I advocate using contractors as a band-aid.

Rushing a hire is but one of the mistakes we see hiring managers make. Other mistakes include pushing the entire hiring process to an individual other than the manager, allowing psychological profiling to completely eclipse the judgment of the hiring team, and allowing the outgoing incumbent (the employee in the job currently) to manage the entire process.

There are many times when I want to force the MATCH hiring process on a hiring manager. After all, with talent as the number one determinant of a company's success, and a proven method for finding and aligning talent with business objectives, I ask, how can it not make sense to implement MATCH? But as my mom always told me, "You can lead a horse to water, but you can't make him drink."

A Lesson Learned

A few years ago I got a call from a business owner. He was a former GE exec who got the entrepreneurial bug and decided to buy an established business. Six months after buying the company, he decided it was time to hire a controller.

He ran an ad in the paper. I saw the ad and called him, asking if he needed my assistance in the hire. He was cordial but clear that he didn't want to pay the fee. I told him that I certainly understood—I wouldn't want to pay a recruiting fee either. After all, we are expensive.

I wished him well and followed up by sending my card and a note. Several years later, I heard back from him. He had been through three controllers and was tired of it. He was ready to give me a try.

So I went down to his facility. I spent hours talking to him about his company as well as the role the controller would play. We walked the grounds. I met all his right-hand employees. I saw the place where the controller would be sitting. We went to lunch and completed the competency profile.

We thoroughly discussed the mission of his organization. We discussed his personal mission as well. When I left, I had a very clear idea of the controller that he wanted and needed.

I came back to the office and compiled the job description. After a few tweaks to the description, we entered into the recruiting phase. After two weeks we arranged for three interviews to be held at our offices. Two of the candidates were asked to come back to interview at the actual work site.

We had thoroughly checked references. Both of the candidates who were being considered had weaknesses, but each candidate also brought many strengths to the table. We were able to compare each candidate, and, through this process, the business owner asked one of the candidates to dinner. The next day, an offer was made and accepted.

Two years later, this controller has become this business's top employee. He is an extension of the mission of the company.

Further, I often get referrals from the business owner, who was originally apprehensive about the value a recruiting firm can offer.

Everyone has the same number of hours in a day to either achieve greatness or screw things up. Your focus, decision making, and actions will determine your level of success. What MATCH says, in effect, is that you should *focus* on your mission and on the importance of hiring the best people into your company. The MATCH process is worth your time. *Invest your time, your energy, and your passion* to bring in the best people. Used effectively, this is one investment that pays huge dividends every time in increased productivity and profitability.

A Word about Contractors

Try Before You Buy

Consider this: according to the National Association of Temporary and Staffing Services (NATSS), more than half of temporary contract assignments last more than 11 weeks. More than 1 in 10 last longer than a year.

Gone are the days when companies just "need a warm body to fill in until Mildred gets back from Orlando." Companies are using contract help strategically, to complete specific projects and to manage the regular overflow of work. In my experience, about one third of contract hires eventually become full-time employees.

The role of the internal contractor impacts today's hiring trends. Project-based accounting and financial professionals are now handling extremely complex work. While the temporary accounts payable clerk is certainly still a standard, it is no longer unusual to bring in a contractor to handle mergers and acquisitions, Securities and Exchange Commission (SEC) reporting, or forecasting. While this may be slightly more expensive on an hourly rate, a contractor's flexibility allows the department to expertly handle more work without having to add a permanent staff member.

The Benefits

The fee for a contract employee is an hourly rate. You are billed only for the hours the employee works. The contract employee is on the staffing firm's payroll, and they are therefore responsible for unemployment and payroll taxes. In most cases, employers can hire a contract employee onto their payroll at any time. The conversion fee varies according to compensation and length of assignment.

The use of contractors attributes to company profitability because of the flexibility they provide.

Many clients are pleasantly surprised at the pedigree of contractor talent that is available. Even if you do not regularly use a recruiter for full-time positions, you may find it worth your while to talk to a recruiter or staffing professional regarding contracting solutions. With the need for flexibility, streamlined management of contractors is becoming a necessary part of doing business.

Managing Contractors

While the benefit of hiring a contractor is attaining a degree of flexibility, detriments include a potential lack of loyalty, knowledge, and company ownership. It is therefore very important to work with a reputable placement firm that screens, verifies references, and has the capacity to perform background checks. Work with a staffing professional that you trust in establishing your required criteria before accepting a temporary employee.

A word of caution: don't forget that your contract staff needs supervision. *You* are responsible for monitoring the work that's done by a contractor. While a staffing firm may send you an excellent contractor, most firms are not accountable for work being produced while a candidate is on your site. Supervision by a competent manager is required.

If you have a project that requires a contractor to work unsupervised, then let your staffing firm know that. They will work with you to help find the right solution to your staffing issue.

Sample Documents for Hiring a Controller

ncluded here are examples of three essential documents used in the MATCH hiring process (in this example, for a controller).

1. **Job description.** The title should be an attention grabber that mentions both your type of company and the open position. Follow this title with:
   - The org chart, which allows the candidate to see very quickly where he or she will fit into the organization.
   - A brief description of the company and the primary, initial objectives. This section *must* include the size of the company and the industry.
   - More details of the skills, requirements, and other considerations. In this case, we have also added the salary. Many companies leave the salary off job descriptions. We do see some value in that, but in this case, the position is right in line with market, so no need to downplay it.
2. **Interview questions.** An internally shared series of questions that would be asked to the candidates who are being interviewed. The idea to stress is that each candidate is asked the same questions so that you can compare apples to apples.
3. **Reference call questions.** At least three references should be called for any candidate—in the case of controller, we'd suggest many more. As with the candidate interview questions, the questions should remain consistent for each reference to ensure a consistent comparison.

Sample Job Description

Controller with expected growth to CFO for expanding service organization Seeks Controller with Growth to CFO

Organizational Chart

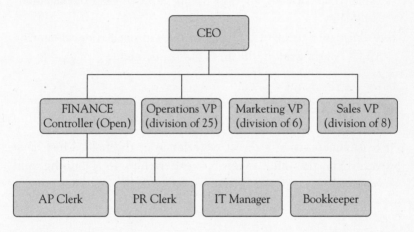

Primary, Initial Objectives of Controller

The controller of this growing $10 million service organization will be responsible for managing the finance division. The first priority will be to streamline the accounting systems. Other duties include implementing an inventory control system. Costs need to be analyzed and contained. Dashboard reports providing quick views of the organization will need to be implemented. The right person in this role will grow to CFO.

Position Description

The controller will report directly to the CEO and will be responsible for the following duties:

1. Establish and maintain the organization's accounting principles, practices, procedures, and initiatives in accordance with GAAP.

2. Prepare financial reports and present findings and recommendations to the management team.
3. Grow and lead a growing accounting department.
4. Implement strategies to increase revenue and decrease costs.
5. Implement cost standards that allow for scalable growth.
6. Develop budgets to map ongoing profitable growth.
7. Keep track of company assets and improve cash management strategies.
8. Advise management on best practices in regards to accounting or CPA firm work in the areas of tax and audit.

Skills/Experience

At least seven years of direct experience in the field. Must have proven expertise and extensive experience in planning and accomplishing corporate goals. A wide degree of creativity is expected.

Requirements/Education

- BS or similar degree in accounting or finance
- CPA preferred

Other Considerations or Preferences

Successful candidates will possess a combination of the following professional characteristics:

- The desire to grow to CFO is a must.
- Strong focus and appreciation of customer service.

Salary

$100,000 to $120,000 + 20 percent bonus

Bonus is subject to company and individual performance—track record of the department indicates a highly probable full bonus potential.

Sample Interview Questions

Note: A typical interview form has three columns: Question, Response, and Comments. Fill out the form during and immediately after the interview. For the sake of saving space, we've shown just the first question in the form. Further, for the sake of this example, I have aligned the skills and competency questions with assumed prioritized areas. As I have noted throughout the book, the MATCH process is designed to produce a customized set of questions for each position. My intent here is simply to show how it all comes together.

Question	Response	Comments
(After initial small talk and ensuring candidate is comfortable)		
1. Please take five minutes and walk me through your career starting with your first job after college, up to today.		

Additional Questions

Let's focus more on your specific skills.

Take me through your experience with:

- Establishing and maintaining an organization's accounting principles, practices, procedures, and initiatives in accordance with GAAP.
- Preparing financial reports and presenting findings and recommendations to your management team.
- Growing and leading a growing accounting department.

- Increasing revenue and decreasing costs.
- Implementing cost standards that allow for scalable growth.
- Developing budgets to map ongoing profitable growth.
- Keeping track of company assets and improving cash management strategies.
- Advising management on best practices in regards to accounting or CPA firm work in the areas of tax and audit.

Now, some general question:

- Describe your ideal job.
- Describe your ideal industry and explain why your strengths match that industry.
- What is your management style?
- Under what type of management are you most effective?
- What has been your best management success?
- In your career, what was your toughest management hurdle, and how did you overcome it?
- How many direct reports do you currently have?
- What size company do you think you'd fit best in and why?
- What size is your current organization?
- Please give me an example of a time where you went above and beyond in the area of customer service.
- What initiative or project were you able to implement that had the biggest impact on the bottom line for your current organization?
- What is the biggest mistake you have ever made in your career?
- What are your greatest strengths? Give me an example of how you apply those strengths.
- What are your greatest weaknesses, and how do you manage those weaknesses?
- If I were to talk to your references, what do you think they would describe as your strengths/weaknesses?
- How do you deal with stress?
- Please give me an example of a time where you allowed stress to get to you at the workplace.
- Describe a recent incident where you encountered a nonperformer. How did you deal with it? What was the outcome?

- What has been the toughest career obstacle you have encountered, and how did you deal with it?
- Who are your career role models and why?
- What is your favorite business book and why?
- If you were hired for this position, what would you do during your first week? Month?
- How do you set goals?
- How many hours per week did you work last year?
- What motivates you?
- What are your long-term goals?

Sample Reference Questions

As with the interview questions, the questions for the candidate's references should have columns for the question, response, and comments. For the sake of saving space, only the first question here is put into the typical format.

Question	Response	Comments
Introduce nature of the call 1. _____ has listed you as a reference, please let me know in what capacity and during what time you had the opportunity to work with _____.		

Additional Questions

Let's focus on specific skills.

Take me through _____'s experience with:

- Establishing and maintaining an organization's accounting principles, practices, procedures, and initiatives in accordance with GAAP.
- Preparing financial reports and presenting findings and recommendations to your management team.

- Growing and leading a growing accounting department.
- Increasing revenue and decreasing costs.
- Implementing cost standards that allow for scalable growth.
- Developing budgets to map ongoing profitable growth.
- Keeping track of company assets and improving cash management strategies.
- Advising management on best practices in regards to accounting or CPA firm work in the areas of tax and audit.

Now, some general questions:

- Describe _____'s ideal job.
- Describe _____'s ideal industry and explain why his/her strengths match that industry.
- What is _____'s management style?
- Please give me an example of a time where _____ went above and beyond in the area of customer service.
- What initiative or project was _____ able to implement that had the biggest impact on the bottom line for his/her current organization?
- What are _____'s greatest strengths? Give me an example of how he/she applies those strengths.
- What are _____'s greatest weaknesses, and how does he/she manage those weaknesses?
- How does _____ deal with stress?
- What motivates _____?
- I am considering hiring _____ as a controller with growth to CFO. In that role, he/she will be doing _____. What are your thoughts on him/her in that role?
- Is there anything else that I should know about?

The Cost of a Mishire

The Story of the Bad Controller

You Know Jack

During his era, Jack Welch was arguably the most effective and respected CEO in business. Consider all the things a CEO has to do. Now consider: Jack Welch bragged that he spent **50 percent** of his time hiring, coaching, and developing his team. That's a lot of man-hours. But that team is what made him so successful. Entrepreneurs have to consider how they spend their time in this regard. The fast-moving small business owner just cannot get by devoting only a minor portion of their time to this important task.

Following is a study we performed on the costs associated with hiring the wrong person. This is a true story, and although just one example, the areas of impact are true for all companies.

Story: The Bad Controller

A client of mine, who is also a friend, called me one day with bad news. She had to fire her controller. She wanted me to help her find a replacement, but in addition, she wanted me to work with her to find out how much this bad controller had cost her company. The results were eye opening. If you're at all a numbers person, you'll love this next part.

The controller had been with the company two years and was forced to resign because of a number of poor business decisions and because he could not manage staff. Here are the costs of that mishire:

1. We first figured out how much it cost to hire the controller:

Recruitment/search fee:	$30,000
Outside testing/profiling:	$ 1,000
HR department time:	$ 8,000
HR department admin:	$ 2,000
Travel costs:	$ 1,000
Time expenses for non-HR personnel:	$ 3,000
Relocation:	$10,000
Total hiring costs:	**$55,000**

2. Then we looked at the total compensation package:

Base ($100,000 × 2 years):	$200,000
Bonuses for all years (15% performance):	$ 32,000
Stock options:	$ 5,000
Benefits:	$ 20,000
Clubs/organizations:	$ 4,000
Car:	N/A
Other forms:	$ 39,000
Total compensation:	**$300,000**

3. Next, we calculated the costs to support the person in the job:

Administrative assistant ($25,000 × 2 years):	$ 50,000
Office rental:	$ 10,000
Furniture, computer, etc:	$ 10,000
Travel (air, food, lodging):	$ 10,000
Training:	$ 10,000
Other:	$ 10,000
Total support:	**$100,000**

4. Then came the total severance package:

Severance:	$ 30,000
Outplacement Counseling fee:	$ 10,000
Costs in negotiating separation:	$ 10,000
Costs in lawsuits:	$ 10,000
Administrative costs:	$ 5,000
Wasted time:	$ 15,000
"Bad press"	$ 5,000
Total severance:	**$90,000**

5. Add to this mistakes/failures and missed and wasted business opportunities:

Mishired three people:	$ 150,000
Impaired customer loyalty:	$ 200,000
Failed to enter new "hot" market:	$ 200,000
Installed the wrong software:	$ 200,000
Launched three "dog" products:	$ 250,000
Total estimated missed and wasted business opportunities:	**$1 million**

Summary

A conservative estimate:

Total hiring cost:	$ 55,000
Total compensation:	$ 300,000
Total support:	$ 100,000
Total severance:	$ 90,000
Total estimated missed and wasted business opportunities:	$1,000,000
Total cost of the mishire:	**$1,545,000**

In this case the estimated cost of the mishire was over 15 times the annual salary of the controller. My friend was beside herself as we stared at this outrageous truth. You can believe that she was much more careful with hiring decisions after this analysis.

Onboarding Checklist

In Step 12 of the MATCH process we performed onboarding. In that chapter, I provided a short onboarding check-list. Here is a more in-depth example:

Prearrival

Task	Who Initiates
Go to HR office to complete W-4, I-9, and personal data form, sign employment application, and receive staff handbook and benefits packet.	Employee
Remind new employee to complete the online benefits enrollment within the first 31 days of employment (Must have ID and password).	Hiring manager
Contact administrative services regarding parking options.	Employee
Introduce to coworkers.	Hiring manager
Distribute assigned key and/or access card to office.	Hiring manager
Discuss procedures for scheduling time off and unexpected absences.	Hiring manager
Review work schedule, pay schedule, and overtime policy (if applicable).	Hiring manager
Review appropriate attire for workplace.	Hiring manager
Go over phones, fax, copier, office supplies.	Peer

Tasks	Who Initiates
Provide computer orientation at desk.	Peer
Give a department tour (place to hang coat, washroom, water fountain, vending machine, pantry/kitchen, refrigerator, emergency exit, parking space).	Peer
Arrange a welcome lunch for new employee.	Hiring manager and/or peer

Within First Week

Tasks	Who Initiates
Activate ID online if you have not done so.	Employee
Sign up for direct deposit and update online directory.	Employee
Review job responsibilities, competencies, and expectations.	Hiring manager
Review performance feedback and appraisal process.	Hiring manager
Review department's mission, strategy, values, functions, policies and procedures; organization of the department; critical members of the department; departmental staff directory, department calendar, confidentiality of information; emergency regulations, health and safety training.	Hiring manager
Review standards for business conduct (nondiscrimination, no smoking, drug and alcohol, no tolerance of workplace violence, sexual harassment prevention and resolution).	Hiring manager
Other workshops and trainings.	Employee

Within Two Weeks

Tasks	Who Initiates
Attend new employee orientation and payroll.	Employee
Schedule weekly or monthly meeting to touch base with supervisor.	Employee
Overview of budget and finance procedures and policies (if applicable).	Hiring manager
Accounting and reporting processes, effective business operations (as applicable).	Hiring manager

First Day

Task	Who Initiates
Enroll for benefits via electronic within 31 days of hire date.	Employee
Review and clarify performance objectives and expectations after the first month.	Hiring manager
Set up brief meeting with department's head.	Hiring manager
Register for new employee orientation, part 2.	Employee

Within First Month

Task	Who Initiates
Attend new employee orientation, part 2.	Employee
Meet fellow new employees.	Employee
Review and discuss the staff member's performance objectives.	Hiring manager

During First 90 Days

Task	Who Initiates
Review performance objectives and progress.	Hiring manager
Discuss training completed and training planned for the future.	Hiring manager

Fifth and Sixth Months

Task	Who Initiates
Conduct annual performance review.	Hiring manager
Set objectives for the coming year with employee.	Hiring manager

Once complete, this checklist should be signed by both the staff member and the supervising staff member. A copy should be provided to the staff member with the original filed in the department staff member's file. Please contact your human resources consultant with any questions.

Staff Member's Name (Please Print) _____

Job Title _____

Hire Date _____

Staff Member's Signature _____ Date _____

Supervising Staff or Faculty Member Signature _____

Date _____

ABOUT THE
AUTHOR

D an Erling is the president of Accountants One, a recruiting firm headquartered in Atlanta, Georgia, and founded in
1973. Dan joined Accountants One in 1998. Since then,
he has helped match over 1,000 companies with exceptional talent.
He specializes in controller, chief financial officer (CFO), vice
presidential (VP), and director-level searches, though his firm is
active across the accounting and financial spectrum.

Throughout his career, Dan has had the honor of serving companies ranging from small start-ups to the largest public companies.
Though much of his work is based in the Southeast, he has extensive experience with both national and international searches.
Over his career, he has done work for companies in such diverse
industries as manufacturing, banking, entertainment, transportation, software, electronics, accounting (CPA firms), construction,
energy, real estate, services, broadcasting, retail, biotechnology,
technology, health care, nonprofits, and automotive.

In Dan's opinion, every hire is crucial to the success of an
organization. His goal is to work with companies who are as passionate as he is about hiring great people. His disarming and down-
to-earth approach provides a nice balance to his relentless drive for
objectively evaluating talent and aligning that talent with his
client's mission.

Dan's career has consisted of only two jobs (ignoring his stints
working in photo labs, movie theaters, and painting houses to put

him through college). His first job, for eight years, was as an inner-city math teacher. He was a good teacher. In fact, in 1996, he was named the Academic Achievement Incentive Teacher of the Year for Middle Schools. He loved teaching children but did not like the public school bureaucracy. Following several summers of working for his dad as the IT Project Manager for Accountants One, Dan signed on full-time.

When Dan arrived, there were three employees at Accountants One. Dan applied his dad's theories of "people first" and "long-term thinking" and soon became the firm's top salesperson. Dan began looking for people who thought in a similar way and soon added to the team (in fact, Dan's first two hires are still with the company). The firm has continued to grow and, in 2008, Accountants One opened its first satellite office in Raleigh, North Carolina.

The financial success of Accountants One has been considerable, but Dan is most proud of the firm's placement success rate. Since he started tracking the firm's direct hire placement success rate, it has never fallen below 91 percent, and for several years it hovered at 98 percent. Even on the contractual side, Accountants One maintains a success rate that is second to none in the placement industry.

Dan is in the Georgia Association of Personnel Services (GAPS) Million Dollar Hall of Fame and is recognized as one of Atlanta's Up and Comers by the *Atlanta Business Chronicle*. Under Dan's leadership, Accountants One was named one of Atlanta's Best Places to Work. He is often quoted as an industry expert and is a requested speaker in the area of hiring best practices—focusing on specific areas or the MATCH process as a whole.

Further, Dan is the creator of the Search for the South's Funniest Accountant (www.accountantsarefunnytoo.com). The philosophy of looking past stereotypes and assumptions permeates this night of hilarious fund raising during which financial professionals compete in an *American Idol* style comedy stand-up competition with a grand prize of an all-expenses paid trip to Las Vegas. The combination fund-raiser/stereotype debunker has become an annual favorite in the accounting community. Over

700 people attend the event, raising over $20,000 for Junior Achievement every year.

Erling earned a Bachelor of Science in Mathematics from Georgia State University and a Masters from Emory University. Mathematics has always been a cornerstone for Dan, as demonstrated by his focus on metrics and objective analysis. By objectively and mathematically analyzing the impact of hiring strategies, Dan developed the MATCH process.

Dan's experience as teacher, mathematician, and executive recruiter intersected to create this book. Over the years, whenever asked to present seminars on specific hiring practices, Dan went through the process of carefully documenting the various hiring strategies he'd encountered. He realized that his role as recruiter and advisor afforded him the ability to evaluate hiring strategies across a wide variety of companies and industries. By methodically evaluating success and failure, Dan's collection of experiences developed into a system of best practices with proven results. The result of this decade of work is the book you have in your hands.

MATCH: A Systematic/Sane Process for Hiring the Right Person Every Time is Dan's first book. He hopes it provides you with great value, but he also recognizes that the process doesn't stop here. Hiring great people—which is any organization's most critical key to success—is not a static discussion. This conversation can go on for a lifetime, and he hopes that you will join in and share your knowledge and experience.

On evenings and weekends Dan writes a blog for his web site: www.danerling.com. The subject matter is usually hiring related— from the philosophical to the ridiculous. Occasionally he'll slip in an entry on funny accountants or even photos from company events. He believes that the overall purpose of his blog is to continue the dialog on hiring best practices.

Dan is also proud to be a minority partner in a staffing firm called The Waters Organization; this sister company to Accountants One specializes in staffing at the administrative level and is run by two long-term employees. Dan is extremely proud of the successes of Waters under the guidance of Melanie Davis and Holly Monaghan.

Recently they were awarded a multi year, multi million-dollar staffing project with one of the largest employers in the state of Georgia.

Recently, Dan lost his dad and business partner. On May 2, 2010, Bert Erling died of a massive heart attack. He was almost 67 years old. Bert was a great accountant, a solid businessman, and a caring man. He believed in people and their ability to form something positive out of whatever the world threw at them. Hence, his favorite saying was, "when life gives you lemons, make lemonade."

Dan is not all business. In fact, on Friday nights you'll find Dan working on his series of abstract paintings called the 7 Rocks Project. He also enjoys tennis and playing the piano.

But most important to Dan is his family. He has two wonderful boys (Nelson and Wren) whose tennis matches and musical concerts he never misses. Michelle, his lovely wife of 19 years, is an educator and a painter, and Dan claims that she is the inspiration for all his work. The whole bunch lives in Atlanta, Georgia, with their two dogs, rabbit, and many tropical fish.

INDEX

AARs. *See* After Action Reviews

Accountants One:
  company description, xx, 2, 213–215
  hiring success rate of, xiii
  recommendation for, xi–xii

After Action Reviews, 175

Atlanta Business Chronicle, 214

Aristotle, 177

Ash, Mary Kay, 137

Baby boomers, 157–159

Background checks. *See* Checks, background

Behavioral interviewing. *See* Interviewing, behavioral

Business objectives, 12–13, 15, 124, 171, 185

Career wound, 115

CEO. *See* Chief Executive Officer

CFO. *See* Chief Financial Officer

Checks, background:
  discussing with candidate, 98, 127
  performing, 128–130

Chief Executive Officer:
  hiring stories involving, ix, 12–13, 31, 86, 202
  in business surveys about hiring, 2
  in organizational chart, 43–44, 195
  role in assuring candidate accepts offer, 144
  role in the hiring process, 27–29, 135–136

Chief Financial Officer:
  hiring stories involving, ix–xii, 75
  in organizational chart, 44–45
  in sample job description, 195–200
  role in onboarding, 149

Collins, Jim, 9, 21, 55

Competency profile:
  creation of, 55–76
  debriefing on, 175
  definition of, 56

Competency profile (*continued*)
  in behavioral interviewing,
      65–74, 116–117
  in prioritizing personality traits,
      63–64
  in self-assessments, 5
  responsibility for, 29
  sample form, 58–63
  value in the hiring decision, 136
Contractors:
  benefits of, 190–191
  in recruiting plan checklist, 79
  managing, 191
  when to use, 185
Controller:
  hiring stories involving, 75–76,
      101, 186, 201–205
  in organizational chart,
      44–45, 195
  in sample interview script,
      115–116
  sample documents for hiring,
      193–200
    interview questions, 197
    job description, 195
    reference questions, 199
Corporate culture (*See also* Hiring,
      culture):
  aligning with recruiting
      approach, 86
  clarifying, 32–38, 174
  impact of, 15, 166
  scorecard to measure, 31, 35–38
Counteroffer. *See* Offer,
      counteroffer
Culture. *See* Corporate culture. *See*
      Hiring, culture

Danerling.com, xiv, 38, 52, 57,
      184, 215

Darwin, Charles, 142
Debrief sessions, 175–176
Decision making, 133
  effect of psychological
      assessments on, 75
  entrepreneurs and, 14
  emotions, role in, 145
  Generation X and, 158
  in competency profile, 58–59,
      63, 68
  in corporate culture
      assessment, 36
  intuition and, 15
  poor, 13,164, 203
  problems with, 14,106, 113
  quotes about, 2, 11–12, 26, 91,
      119, 162
  relationship to mission,
      30, 184
  team roles in, 13, 29,
      134–136
Dilbert, 24
Drucker, Peter, 2, 11, 26, 119,
      146, 183

Employee retention. *See*
      Retention
Entrepreneurs, 14, 202

Fair Credit Reporting Act, 129
Ford, Henry, 155

Generation X, 158
Georgia Association of Personnel
      Services (GAPS), 214
Go forward point, 94 (*see also*
      Knockout point)
Google, 23
Greenspan, Alan, 162
Gut instincts, 14–15

Harley-Davidson, 23, 144
Hiring:
  culture of, 28, 154, 174,
    177–181, 184
  life cycle, xvii
  prioritization of, 2, 10–11, 14, 87
  ROI. *See* Return on Investment
  success rate, xiii, 1, 4–5, 11, 14,
    104, 106, 214
Hiring manager:
  in job overview, 50, 52
  mistakes made by, 14, 57, 104,
    106, 185
  role in hiring process, 78, 92–93,
    98, 121
  role in onboarding, 208–210
  stories involving, 101, 104
Hiring team:
  assembling, 26–31
  meetings, 30, 136, 167,
    173–174, 181
  roles, 13, 28–29, 135
  scorecard and, 34–35
Human resources, 81, 121, 145,
    151, 174
  role in hiring process, 29,
    135–136, 176, 208

Iacocca, Lee, 47
Interviewing:
  behavioral, 65, 66–74
  competency, 64
  face-to-face, 102–118
  format, 104
  inappropriate questions, 94–95
  locations for, 118
  parts of process of, 109–118
  red flags, 115
  sample questions, 66–74,
    197–199

  stories about, 12, 54, 75–76, 79,
    104, 186–187
  telephone. *See* Phone screen
tips, 105–109, 115, 117, 139, 174

Job description, 50
Job overview:
  benefits of, 49
  common mistakes in writing, 54
  parts of, 48
  sample, 52–53

Kaizen, 179–180
Ken Blanchard Companies, 23
King, Billie Jean, 169
Knockout point, 93, 100 (*see also*
    Go forward point)
Knight, Philip, 17
Kravis, Henry, 32, 102

Manager, hiring. *See* Hiring
    manager
Mantra, 21, 87
Maslow, Abraham, 133
McGriff, Fred, 167
Mentoring, 145, 149, 156, 160–161
Mind-set, proper, 9–16, 30, 105
Mishire, cost of, 15, 164, 201–205
Mission:
  assessing, 5
  in recruiting plan, 59, 69
  value of, 15, 27, 179, 181,
    183–184
Mission statement:
  core areas addressed, 21
  Dilbert, humorous, 24–25
  ownership, 22, 209
  purpose, 18–20
  samples, 23, 52
  use in hiring process, 48, 50

Mission statement (*continued*)
  behavioral interviewing, 65
  justifying the position, 30,
    80, 171
  onboarding, 149
  retention, 157, 159

National Association of Temporary
  and Staffing Services, 190
Note taking, 96, 106, 108

Offer:
  acceptance of, 142–145
  counteroffer, 140–141
  extending, 137–141, 171
  helping candidate accept,
    144–145
  knowing what to, 139
  letter, 141
Onboarding:
  checklist, 151–152, 207–211
  effective, 149–150
  performing, 146–152
  phases of, 150
  reasons for, 148–149
Organizational chart:
  creating, 41–46, 194
  evaluating, 174
  questions to candidates
    involving, 69–72
  reasons for, 42–43, 45
  samples, 43–45, 195 (*see also*
    www.danerling.com)

Performers:
  average, 19, 71
  poor, 20, 49, 61, 71–72
  top, 19, 71, 75, 104, 157
Phone screen, 91–101

  conducting, 96
  form for, 93
  objective of, 92
  recruiting firms, use of in, 101
  sample questions, 96–97
  tips, 95–96, 99–100
Psychological assessments,
  74–75, 185

Reagan, 128
Recruiters, external, 80–81, 85
  developing relationship with, 88
  use in phone screen process, 101
  view from inside, 184–185
Recruiting methods, 83–87
Recruiting plan:
  checklist for, 79–81
  hiring team roles in, 29
implementing, 89
  preparing, 40
  review of, 175
  structuring, 77–88
References:
  checking, 119–127
  getting calls returned, 125
  sample call scripts, 98, 122–124
  sample questions, 199–200
  value of, 112, 126–127
Retained search firm. *See*
  Recruiters, external
Retention:
  generational motivation,
    157–158
  improving, 19, 150, 157
  key areas of, 159
  strategies for, 160–161
Return on investment:
  areas to measure, 164–165,
    167–168

role of hiring team, 28–29
testing, 162–168
Revenue-per-employee (RPE), 165
Ritz-Carlton, 22–24
ROI. *See* Return on investment

Search for the South's Funniest
    Accountant, 214
Securities and Exchange
    Commission (SEC), 53, 190
Seven rocks project, 216
Skills,
    advertising, 75
    confirming (*see* References,
        checking)
    developing candidate's, 159–160
    evaluating, 54, 79, 94–95, 105,
        109, 112
    gaps in, 147, 150
    hard (*see* Skills, required)

interpersonal, 109
interviewing (*see* Interviewing,
    face-to-face)
required, 48, 51
examples, 53, 111, 196
sample questions about, 97,
    110–111, 115–116,
    197–200
soft (*see* competency profile)
Sloan, Jr., Alfred P., 41
Smart, Bradford D., 63
Southwest Airlines, 23

Telephone screen. *See* Phone
    screen

Walt Disney Company, 23
Waters Organization, xiii, xv, 2,
    215
Welch, Jack, 11, 91, 202